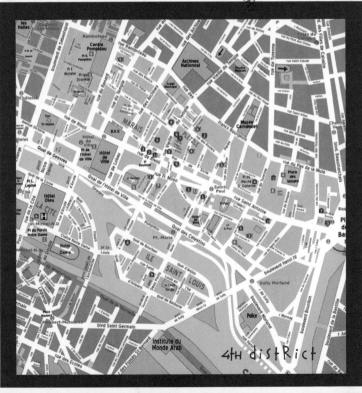

4TH disTRict

JUNIOR Jetsetters™
guide to
PARIS

Junior Jetsetters™ Guide to Paris
First edition February 2009
ISBN-13: 978-0-9784601-4-3

Published in Toronto by Junior Jetsetters Inc.
3044 Bloor St. W., Suite 550, Toronto, ON M8X 2Y8 (Canada)
Text: Pedro F. Marcelino, Slawko Waschuk
Sub-Editor: Anna Humphrey
Characters: Kim Sokol
Illustrations: Miguel Vieira da Silva (www.miguelv.com)
Cover Design: Pedro F. Marcelino, set in Casual Font by A.J. Palmer
Cover Art: Miguel Vieira da Silva, Tapan Gandhi (logo), Kim Sokol (stamp).

Special Thanks to: Xanita Mendes, Sheridan College Institute of Technology.

Library and Archives Canada Cataloguing in Publication

Marcelino, Pedro F., 1978-
     Junior Jetsetters guide to Paris / Pedro F. Marcelino, Slawko
Waschuk ; edited by Anna Humphrey ; illustrated by Kim Sokol,
Miguel Vieira da Silva and Tapan Gandhi.

ISBN 978-0-9784601-4-3

     1. Paris (France)--Guidebooks--Juvenile literature.
I. Waschuk, Slawko, 1974- II. Humphrey, Anna, 1979- III. Sokol, Kim,
1987- IV. Vieira da Silva, Miguel, 1976- V. Gandhi, Tapan, 1986-
VI. Title. VII. Title: Guide to Paris.

DC708.M37 2009   j914.4'3610484   C2008-907853-5

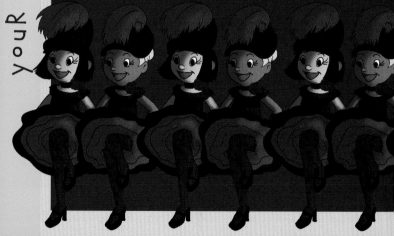

out-of-town and fuRthER afiELd

what do you know about paris?

Paris is the capital of France and one of the largest cities in Europe. It's a world-famous destination with a rich history, and it's filled with unforgettable attractions, buildings and events. Everyone knows the Eiffel Tower—which has become, not only the symbol of Paris, but of France, too—but it's only the beginning of what's in store for you here. You'll find countless museums and amusement parks to visit, parks to stroll through, tours to take and landmarks to see. With all of this going for it, is it any wonder Paris is one of the most popular places in the world to visit?

how cool is that?

Paris is actually relatively flat—the terrain changes less than the height of a ten-storey building (if you exclude Montmartre and Belleville). This amazing city is home to the Louvre, the world's largest museum, which was built over hundreds of years, and has hosted some of the most famous artists in the world, particularly Impressionists.

The River Seine has always been a key inspiration for them and is the real heart and soul of Paris. The city is divided into 20 districts (called *arrôndissements*), which are numbered in a spiral fashion, looking a bit like a snail. It starts with the oldest area of the city (*1er.*, or first district). It's in the city centre, by the river. Then it works its way around. The beautiful River Seine is also a big part of why Paris is often called the City of Love. Younger Parisians just nicknamed their city Paname. However, its world-renown moniker is really another: the City of Light. You'll see why when you go on a night-time river cruise with your parents!

a little History

way back, even before your granny was born, there were these people called the parisii

In 250 BC a Celtic tribe settled in the area now known as Paris. They were called the Parisii. The huge area around this settlement was known as Gaul, and was made up of parts of today's France, Belgium, Switzerland, the Netherlands, Germany and Italy. The area was highly sought-after, especially by the Romans, who eventually took it for themselves. They named the Paris area Lutetia (*Lutèce* in French) and the town prospered. Today there are still remnants of these Roman times, like the Arènes de Lutèce (Lutetia Arena) and the Thermes de Cluny (the Gallo-Roman Baths in the Museum of the Middle Ages). Over the next few centuries, Gaul was invaded again and again. At one point, Lutetia was destroyed. Because of this, the Île de la Cité was eventually fortified for protection from future attacks. It was at about this time that it started to be called Paris.

Kings showed up and Ruled away

The attacks continued and, in 486, a king named Clovis took over the city of Paris, and then went on to conquer big parts of Gaul. He started the Merovingian dynasty— the first family of kings of France. The Merovingians were later replaced by the Carolingians, whose first king was called Pippin (like the guy in *The Lord of the Rings*). His son, Charlemagne, is often considered the forefather of the idea of a united Europe, since he conquered and united most of Western Europe during his reign.

paRis bEcamE a capital city

The next to rule were the Capetians. Up until this time, Paris wasn't considered the 'capital' of the kingdom. But, under the Capetians, the government became much more complicated and it needed a permanent home. So Paris became the main home of the king and the capital of the country. It was during this time that Notre Dame and the original markets of Les Halles were built. Soon after, the Conciergerie and Sainte-Chapelle (ordered by Louis IX) were built. The Châteaus of Fontainebleau and Vincennes were also built around this time and were popular retreats for the kings.

tHERE was waR foR 100 yEaRs!

Things took a turn for the worse in 1328. The last of the Capetian kings died, and a battle for the kingdom began the Hundred Years War between France and England. It was a difficult and expensive war, and the French were often defeated. For a while, King Henry VI of England also became king of France. Within a few years, and with the help of Joan of Arc, Charles VII resumed the French throne. Unfortunately, Joan of Arc was betrayed by fellow Frenchmen and was handed over to the English, who burned her as a witch.

tHE plaguE plaguEd tHE pEoplE

The Black Death (also called the Plague) was spreading throughout Europe at this time. The lucky ones who weren't infected had their own worries—food shortages, high taxes, riots and violence were just a few of them. It was really not a nice time to be living in Paris, you know...? Most people were just concerned with their survival in a dirty, smelly, dangerous and violent city!

tHE RENaiSSaNcE flouRisHEd

When the war finally ended, the ruling kings encouraged massive building projects in France and the Renaissance flourished. Under François I, Fontainebleau and the Louvre were transformed into magnificent palaces to promote the works of artists like Leonardo Da Vinci.

it's Not Easy (oR REwaRdiNG) to plEasE GREEks aNd tRojaNs...

Religion was a big issue at the time, and as the Protestant movement entered France, conflict between the Catholics and the Protestants grew. The Bourbons were the next ruling monarchs of France. The first king was Henry IV, who tried to help Catholics and Protestants get along by declaring both religions equal. But the idea was unpopular with both sides, and it eventually led to his assassination (after 23 failed attempts!).

a SuN KiNG bRiGhtENEd tHE couRt

After Henry's death, Cardinal Richelieu ran the country for King Louis XIII with a strong hand. He helped strengthen the monarchy and was responsible for the construction of many new buildings. When King Louis XIV succeeded to the throne, he demanded absolute power and was known as *le Roi Soleil* (Sun King), believing that everything should revolve around him, the way everything revolves around the sun. He ordered many of the greatest monuments you'll see in Paris today. But the period after the his reign was one of turmoil and change. More and more people were able to read and as the publishing industry grew, more educated people began to question the absolute power that the monarchy held. Things were about to get crazy.

tHE fRENcH REvolutioN totally REvolutioNiZES tHE woRld

The French public revolted by storming and burning down the Bastille prison. This event was the start of the French Revolution that pitted the French people against the monarchy, the nobility and the church. A particularly violent part of the revolution is known as the Reign of Terror. Many people were executed by guillotine then— for example, Louis XVI and his wife Marie-Antoinette. The French Revolution lasted about ten years.

NapoléoN madE HimSElf EmpéRoR

At the time, a young officer of the revolution made his way through the ranks to become a military and political leader. His name was Napoléon Bonaparte. He staged a coup d'état (a sudden overthrow of a government) and proclaimed himself Emperor. He waged wars on many countries, including Austria, Italy, Egypt and Russia, and defeated almost all of them. He had way less luck in Portugal, and across Europe the Russians defeated his army big time. Napoléon's army, marching mostly on foot, was attracted to Russia during a terrible winter, and many died on the way. Napoléon was finally exiled from France. After a failed attempt to regain control at the Battle of Waterloo, Napoléon was imprisoned and then exiled to the remote island of Saint Helena (in the Atlantic Ocean), where he eventually died.

MoNaRcHy was REStoREd...soRt of

After living through a violent revolution and then control under Napoléon's dictatorship, the people decided that maybe a monarchy wasn't so bad after all, and they decided to give it another try. The King, however, would have less power than before. This revised system didn't last very long, with several kings giving up the throne! In 1848, Louis Bonaparte (Napoléon Bonaparte's nephew) was elected president of the Second Republic.

a diffERENt NapolEoN took ovER

In 1852, Louis Napoléon declared himself Emperor Napoléon III. During his reign Paris was transformed into the city it is today. Not only were the big streets and avenues built but so were railway stations, new sewer and water systems and many hospitals. A lot was planned by Baron Haussman (you'll see his name all over!). The Franco-Prussian War of 1870 happened under Napoléon III's watch. The French were defeated and Napoléon III was tragically captured. The war continued until a treaty was finally signed.

la bEllE EpoquE bEGaN

The next period, part of which is known as the *Belle Époque* (Beautiful Era), saw a lot of developments in Paris. The Eiffel Tower was built and so was the first subway line. In 1914, war broke out. Paris was close to German occupation, but was able to avoid it. In 1919, several peace treaties were signed after the end of World War I. One of these was the Treaty of Versailles, which was signed at the French château. In the following years, happy about the end of the war, writers and artists flocked to the city, mostly to Montmartre, making it once again the creative centre of Europe.

woRld waR 2: paRis uNdER siEGE

In 1939, Germans, under the orders of Adolf Hitler, once again invaded France and occupied Paris. The city was

13

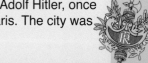

mostly left untouched during the war, but the people weren't as lucky. Caving in to pressure from Germany, the divided government of France began sending Jews to internment camps and ultimately to their deaths. In 1944, after D-Day, Allied Forces liberated Paris, marching through the Arc de Triomphe to the cheering of the crowd.

France and Germany promised each other to be peaceful at last

After Germany's surrender, a new constitution was created. Life in Paris returned to normal pretty quickly, but the war pains were felt for a long time. To prevent any more wars between France and Germany, their leaders decided to co-operate instead of competing. The European Coal and Steel Community was formed. It included France, Germany, Italy, and Benelux (Belgium, the Netherlands and Luxembourg). Years later, the Treaty of Rome marked the beginning of the European Economic Community (EEC), which, in 1993, would become the European Union, with 27 countries today! The goal is to foster friendship and co-operation and ensure that such a war never happens again.

France got another 1st president

In 1959, Charles de Gaulle was elected as the first president of France's Fifth Republic. Many of the presidents, whose names are all still heard in Paris, helped to update the city. De Gaulle's successor, Georges Pompidou, was responsible for the Centre Pompidou, La Villette and Tour Montparnasse. The fourth president, François Mitterrand's contributions included the Louvre's glass pyramid, the La Défense area, the Opéra

14

Bastille and the National Library of France. Jacques Chirac, once mayor of Paris, was the fifth president. The sixth, and current president is Nicolas Sarkozy. He's married to the famous French-Italian singer, Carla Bruni.

paRis today

Today, Paris is one of the most vibrant and exciting cities in the world. From fashion shows to sporting events, there's always something going on. The city's central location also helps to make it a hot spot. Using the TGV (*train à grande vitesse*, French for 'high-speed train') people can travel from the outskirts of France into the city of Paris in just a couple of hours, at the speed of 320 km/h (200 mph). And once you're in the city, getting around is just as easy. Take the Métro to get just about anywhere, or try travelling by boat. You can hop on and off like you would on a bus! There's always something to do and somewhere to go!

GEt REady foR youR tRip!

For more information, visit the Paris Convention and Visitors Bureau site (www.parisinfo.com), where you can learn all about the museums, monuments, shopping, cafés and events in the city. You can also get further information from the City's website (www.paris.fr). If you're going to visit many of the museums and attractions in this guide, consider picking up The Paris Pass (www.paris-pass.com). This pass, which gives you access to many attractions, also lets you skip the lineups and can be used as a Métro pass for public transportation.

If you have any tips or questions for Junior Jetsetters, email us at: **FEEDBACK@JUNIORJETSETTERS.COM** .

HÉLOÏSE LE HARE

bRigittE LE FRENCH poodlE

KEiRa

bastiEN LE badgER

GAËLLE LE GOOSE

PiERRE
LE PEacock

bRuNo
LE black bEaR

joRdi

oNE paRt aquaRium, oNE paRt moviE tHEatRE, all paRts cool

Trust us, you've never seen anything quite like Cinéaqua before! This aquarium is home to 25 sharks and more than 10,000 fish in 43 tanks and aquariums—but that's not all. Movie screens are also placed throughout the space, showing family films, cartoons and environmental movies.

You can also visit the Movieum section (part movie theatre, part museum) for a behind-the-scenes look at filmmaking. You'll learn how to use an aquatic camera, play with real creature animatronics, record and mix audio, and more! There's also a 3-D cinema, a toon tank and a green screen with which you can experiment.

Cinema and sea life are themes throughout Cinéaqua, as is Jules Verne (the French author who wrote *Twenty Thousand Leagues Under the Sea*). Before you leave, be sure to create your own cartoon and post it online, then stop by the touch pool for your chance to touch koï carp and other sturgeon. They love to suck on your fingers, but won't bite you.

cool, yEaH?

All the fish at Cinéaqua come only from France or from French territories around the world.

Jules Verne, who is often called the 'Father of Science Fiction', also wrote Journey to the Center of the Earth, From the Earth to the Moon and Around the World in Eighty Days—all of them really advanced sci-stories, full of gadgets such as aircrafts, submarines and space travel way before they were even invented!

JUNIOR TOP 5 JETSETTERS

18

tHE MoSt faMoUS MoNUMEnt iN tHiS woRld aNd bEyoNd

When the Eiffel Tower was built for Expo 1889, it was only meant to stand for 20 years. Luckily, though, the city decided to keep it. Can you imagine Paris without the Eiffel Tower? Neither can we! Not only is it the tallest building in Paris (it stands over 300 metres or 1,000 feet high), it's also the most recognizable monument in the world!!

The tower was built by Gustave Eiffel, a French structural engineer and architect who also designed the inside of the Statue of Liberty. At the time it was built, many Parisians criticized the tower and its shape, but the reason for Mr. Eiffel's strange choice was actually a technical one—it had to be built to withstand the wind. There are three levels that you can visit: the first floor at 57 metres has a cinema, café, restaurant and outdoor gallery; the second floor at 115 metres has observation decks, a buffet and a souvenir shop; and the top level at 324 metres has an open-air deck, an indoor gallery and a tribute to Gustave Eiffel. Pick up a children's game book at Cineiffel and discover the history of the Eiffel Tower while you follow Gus (in the drawing below) and solve the fun clues in your booklet. Look for a book with Gus on the cover and you're well on your way to be a Paris know-it-all!

cool, yEah?

Hold on tight! Wind and heat sometimes cause the top of the tower to move just a bit!

The Eiffel tower was originally planned to be built for the Universal Exposition of 1888 in Barcelona.

21

cool, yEaH?

Today the museum has over 300,000 relics, some as old as 8,000 years!

During his reign, Napoléon Bonaparte renamed the Louvre after himself! He called it the Musée Napoléon. Talk about self-absorbed!

JUNIOR
TOP 5
JETSETTERS

COME GIVE MONA LISA A SMILE

The Louvre is the biggest museum in the world. It's so big, in fact, that it would take you months to see everything! So, just tell your parents to relax, pick one area that you all like, and take your time. After all, you can come back. The Louvre has been here for 800 years. It's probably not going anywhere.

Like many buildings in Paris, the Louvre didn't start out as a museum. King Philippe II first built it as a fortress to defend the banks of the River Seine. In the 14th century, it was made into a grand castle. In the 16th century, King François I demolished it and began constructing a new palace in the Renaissance style. Construction of the palace continued for the next 300 years, with new kings adding sections, and the Louvre was used as royal residence until King Louis XIV chose Versailles as the new seat of the crown (SEE page 174). King Louis XIV's successors went on to turn part of the palace into a public museum displaying some of the royal collection, but the building didn't fully become a museum until the French Revolution. At that time, a lot of the art displayed was confiscated from churches and royal properties. In the 1980s, a new addition was made to the museum. You can't miss the big glass pyramid in the courtyard. You might remember it from *The Da Vinci Code*!

The most famous work in the Louvre is, of course, Leonardo Da Vinci's Mona Lisa. Unless you come first thing in the morning, be prepared to wait in line for this little one! There are three main wings in the museum: Sully, Denon and Richelieu: Sully contains artifacts from ancient Egypt and Greece and is the place to see the remnants of the original fortress; Denon features Italian art; and Richelieu European and French art.

tHE woRld's gRandEst cathEdRal

Notre Dame Cathedral isn't the biggest cathedral in the world (Seville in Spain, takes that honour) but it's easily the most famous and the most recognizable. And it's definitely the masterpiece of the Gothic period. It took a whopping two centuries to build—from 1163 to 1345. The two towers are 69 metres high, and the church is 130 metres long. One-thousand three-hundred large trees were cut down to build the structure. If the building already looks familiar to you, it's probably because this is the second most famous landmark in Paris (right after the Eiffel Tower). It's also featured in a really famous book (and movie), called *Notre Dame de Paris* or *The Hunchback of Notre Dame*, by Victor Hugo. The main character is Quasimodo, a hunchback who lives hidden from the world up in the towers, peering down from between two gargoyles. His love for a gypsy girl called Esmeralda made theirs a favourite love story. The cathedral is famous for its rose windows and for the sculptures of gargoyles and other monsters that look down on passers-by, protecting the

cool, yEah?

Notre Dame's 130-metre length and its imposing height make it so large that you could fit an entire football stadium inside, with a bit of pacience!!

France's Kilometre Zero is marked with a star on the pavement, in front of the main door. That means every place in France is a certain distance away from Notre Dame.

24

church. Climbing the towers is a challenge. There are many steps, and the stairwell is kind-of narrow and claustrophobic. But if you can get through it, you'll get a beautiful view of Paris. One tip: try to get there really early to avoid lining up for hours and to enjoy the view without dozens of tourists jostling for space.

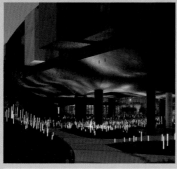

cool, yEah?

As it turns out, the museum's scientists found out the crystal skull was a fake. Specialists say the workmanship is too perfect, and no human being could have made it with any instrument. Human or alien? You decide.

Thousands of the museum's weird musical instruments reserve is inside a glass dome at the entrance. Come close to the glass. Do you hear the musical 'whispering'?

tHE MoSt MYStERiouS quay

Are you totally bored of visiting museums, yet? Even if you are, don't skip this one. Not only does it have the most amazing collection, but the building itself is one of the coolest you'll ever see. If you went up to the top of the Eiffel Tower, you probably looked down and saw a weird building with things sticking out, colourful boxes of different sizes, a vertical garden, a horizontal garden that looks like a messy puzzle, metal beams floating off the third floor, and a huge glass wall separating the street from the museum grounds.

That's the Musée du Quai Branly—and it only gets weirder once you get inside. A wacky path takes you upstairs where you'll find yourself in a labyrinth! There are narrow, dimly lit corridors darting out in every direction to the different artifacts. If you get lost, don't worry. That's supposed to happen! The architect—Mr. Jean Nouvel—designed the building this way because he wanted visitors to feel like they were lost among other cultures. Here, you'll find arts and crafts from civilizations in Asia, Africa, Oceania and the Americas. The former President Jacques Chirac, assembled works from several museums to make up the large collection you'll see. His aim was to make Quai Branly a place of understanding and sharing between all cultures.

At the museum all things look strange and alien, and the artifacts you see aren't always explained clearly, but that's part of the mystery and the fun. You'll find the audio tour fun to do, but it might leave you feeling even more curious about what you're seeing. Some pieces are way-cool: when we visited they had Indiana Jones's crystal skull. Yeah, *that* crystal skull! Be sure to check out the spectacular exhibits up in the mezzanines! (You'll see your parents lost like lab rats downstairs...!)

wHaT's tHE StatuE of libERty doiNG iN paRis !?!?

The Île des Cygnes is a long, narrow artificial island in the River Seine, between the Champs de Mars Park and Javel. It was originally meant to protect the port of Grenelle. Today, there's a walkway along the entire length of the island, named l'Allée des Cygnes (Swan Boulevard). And at the very end of the island stands a replica of the Statue of Liberty. What, you might be wondering, is the Statue of Liberty doing outside America?? Well, French citizens living in the US gave the statue to France for the 100-year anniversary of the French Revolution. The statue originally faced the Eiffel Tower, with its back to the US, but it was later turned around during the Expo of 1937. You can walk all the way there if you want to… but to see the statue properly you have to be inside a boat heading toward the Eiffel Tower!

In any case, the Allée des Cygnes is worth a visit on its own. While most people stick to the two main islands upstream, the fact that you can see both banks of the Seine from this one makes it special. A total of three bridges intersect it, so it's also quite the position for train and boat enthusiasts! On your way back, a brief walk around Bir Hakeim station is perfect to do some colourful grafitti spotting as well. We suggest you take the Métro towards Passy—you get to see the island from above!

28

cool, yeah?

The island is about 850 metres long and only 11 metres wide, at its widest point, so you can see both sides of the river at any time!

This Statue of Liberty of Paris is only a quarter of the height of the original in the US.

tHE MyStERiEs of tHE dEEp bluE

Outside Paris, not far from Disneyland Paris Resort, you'll find Aquarium Sea Life. It's the largest aquarium in the area, with over 300 species in 50 different tanks. You can discover the mysteries of the deep blue waters of the world at this interactive aquarium that combines modern technology, glass displays and marine education. Although it's involved in marine conservation and awareness-raising, the aquarium also puts on a great and entertaining exhibit.

The newest display is Amazonie. There, you'll discover the creatures that live in the waters of the dense forests and mangroves, like piranhas and stingrays. The aquarium also has loads of sharp-teeth sharks, evil-looking moray eels, multi-armed octopuses, and an army of tropical fish and sea turtles.

One of the best occasions to learn all about the world's oceans is during the scheduled feeding demonstrations (look them up as soon as you get there) and don't leave before checking out the touch pools, where you can actually touch the fish... Slimy? A little, but definitely cool.

cool, yEah?

Fish have been on earth for more than 450 million years. They were around even before dinosaurs!!

The largest fish is the great white shark which can grow to 15 metres (50 feet) in length.

cool, yEah?

The 21 partner Arab member countries are: Algeria, Bahrain, Djibouti, Egypt, Iraq, Jordan, Kuwait, Lebanon, Libya, Mauritania, Morocco, Oman, Palestine, Qatar, Saudi Arabia, Somalia, Sudan, Syria, Tunisia, United Arab Emirates and Yemen.

Indonesia, with 222 million people, is the 4th most populated country in the world, and the largest Muslim majority (but it isn't an Arab country).

a SpacE-aGE buildiNG RiGHt oN tHE RivERsidE

Who do you think about when you hear the words 'Arab' or 'Muslim'? To a lot of people, the meanings of the words are confusing. 'Arab' is the dominant culture in the region called the Middle East and in parts of North Africa, where most people speak Arabic as either their first or second language. 'Muslim' is a religion or faith that is practised in different parts of the world. France has one of the biggest Arab and/or Muslim populations in today's Europe, and the Paris region is home to most of them.

The Arab World Institute was created as a place for 21 Arab-speaking countries and France to come together. These countries manage this space, organizing concerts and exhibits about themes related to the Arab world and France, always with a modern spin. It's a wonderful chance to learn about one of the great cultures of the world. You can even take home some music and books from the store… that is, if you can read Arabic, which is written from right to left!

The coolest thing about the institute is its building, its location, and how open the space is to the public. An architect called Jean Nouvel designed it for a site on the banks of the Seine. It is clad in reflective silvery glass panels, inside of which metal screens interact individually to the amount of sunlight, opening and closing as needed, to control the environment inside! Outside the building, there's a large plaza that looks like an Arab square. People love to come by at lunchtime to hang out and eat their baguettes.

معهد العالم العربي

33

cool, yEaH?

One of France's veterans associations relights the memorial flame every day at 6:30 pm.

There are 284 stairs up to the top of the Arc de Triomphe.

34

aN aRc to HoNouR soldiERs aNd cRazy tRaffic jaMs

Napoléon Bonaparte (Napoléon I) was a powerful force in Europe. He led his troops to battle against Italy, Egypt, Austria, Spain, Portugal, Poland and Russia. As an honour to his *Grande Armée* (the Great Army), Napoléon ordered a monument to be built in the Place de l'Étoile. Construction was slow. It began in 1806, but by 1810 only the foundation had been completed. The power of the army decreased and, when it was defeated by Russia it started a disastrous downturn. The final defeat came in 1815 at the Battle of Waterloo, in today's Belgium.

Construction of the Arc was put on hold until King Louis-Philippe ordered it to be completed. He then got permission to bring Napoléon's remains back to France. During a grand procession in 1840, Napoléon's ashes passed through the Arc on their way to Les Invalides, where his tomb stands today. In the years since it was completed, several victory marches have gone past the Arc, including the Germans in 1871, the French in 1918, the Germans in 1940 and the French and their allies in 1944–1945. After World War I, to honour *all* soldiers who gave their lives for their country, the Unknown Soldier was symbolically buried beneath the Arc, where a flame is lit every day.

The Arc stands in Paris's most famous traffic circle, known as Étoile–or 'star'–because 12 important avenues depart from it. Traffic jams in this roundabout are legendary and absolutely insane! The best place to watch them is up there from the Arc's rooftop… but you have to climb hundreds of stairs to get there. Yeah, good things won't come easy... But this one is totally worth the effort, as you get an eagle-eye view of Paris!

mEGa-muSEum of iNtERioR stylE

Over a hundred years ago, several art collectors got together and formed an organization. Today it's a museum complex called Les Arts Décoratifs with several distinct museums: Musée des Arts Decoratifs, Musée de la Mode et du Textile, Musée de la Publicité and Musée Nissim de Camondo. Some of them are located within the Louvre.

The Musée des Arts Decoratifs (Museum of Decorative Arts) is all about interior styles over the centuries. It has furniture, carpets, art, wallpaper, ceramics, toys and more. The period rooms are really interesting. They recreate typical rooms from different times, all the way back to the Middle Ages. If you've ever thought that it would be cool to live back then, check out what your room might have looked like. It's probably not what you'd expect.

The Musée de la Mode et du Textile focuses on textiles such as silk, cotton, lace, embroidery, clothes and costumes. The Musée de la Publicité is an advertising museum, with posters and advertisements from film, newspapers, magazines and radio. The Musée Nissim de Camondo is an actual house that was donated to Les Arts Décoratifs with furniture from the 17th and 18th centuries.

cool, yEaH?

Are you wondering why some of the beds in Musée des Arts Décoratifs are so short? People used to sleep almost sitting up back in the 15th century, supposedly because they were afraid of dying with a rush of blood to their heads!

The Galerie de Jouets (toy gallery) has over 12,000 toys.

cool, yEah?

The first successful manned flight in a hot-air balloon took off from the property in 1783.

Bois de Boulogne is 2.5 times larger than Central Park in New York, and 3.3 times larger than Hyde Park in London.

a Royally Good GEtaway!

Bois de Boulogne used to be a forest where kings hunted wolves, deer and boar. It became a park in 1852 when Napoléon III decided to make it one. The result of his planning was a park with a combination of roads, lawns, forests, lakes and waterfalls. It looked a little bit like Hyde Park, which Napoléon had seen during his exile in London.

Today, it's nothing like that original royal hunting forest, but you won't even miss the wild boar! There's tons of stuff to do in this huge park. Rent a bicycle if you want to see everything! Paddleboats are available at the Lac Inférieur, or you can bring a remote-controlled boat and sail it around in the Lac Supérieur. The park contains two horse racetracks (the Hippodrome de Longchamp and Hippodrome d'Auteuil), a museum, a bird sanctuary, flower gardens and restaurants. The Jardin d'Acclimatation, an amusement park just for kids (SEE paGE 68), is also in the park.

oNE GiaNt paRK aNd about 10 miLLioN tHiNGS to do iN it...

Like the Bois de Boulogne, the Bois de Vincennes was once a hunting ground for the kings of France. And, like the Bois de Boulogne, the Bois de Vincennes was made into a public park by Napoléon III.

These days, Bois de Vincennes is landscaped with lakes and stuffed full of things to see and do, like paddleboats, a zoo (SEE paGE 132), sports venues of all sorts, biking lanes, sidewalks, a bird sanctuary, a baseball field, soccer fields, a horse racing track, a farm and a Buddhist temple.

The Parc Floral de Paris (Paris Flower Park), located in the Bois de Vincennes, is a well-known botanic garden with its own amusement park. Over 3,000 flower varieties are mixed with sculptures, games, a miniature golf course, a merry-go-round and a puppet theatre. It's probably one of the most fun places to go in Paris.

cool, yEaH?

King Louis IX dispensed justice under a huge oak tree in the park, or so the legend says!

The park's Château de Vincennes once held an important religious relic, while Sainte-Chapelle (SEE paGE 58) was being built. That relic was allegedly Jesus Christ's Crown of Thorns.

41

bRidgE-hoppiNg iN tHE sEiNE

Because the River Seine goes right through the centre of the city, Paris is full of bridges. There are 37 of them in total, and each one has its own history! There are lots of impressive ones, but a few of them are especially interesting and shouldn't be missed. A boat or walking tour is just the right way to see them all!

The Pont-Neuf is the oldest bridge in Paris but, at the time it was built, over 400 years ago, it was the newest. Before then, bridges were mostly made of wood and often didn't last long. But Pont-Neuf, built of stone, remains. It was also the first bridge in Paris that did not have houses built on it. The Pont Alexandre III might be the most beautiful Parisian bridge. Built for the Universal Exposition of 1900, the bridge is decorated with elaborate lampposts and sculptures. Each end also has tall pillars with large golden statues.

The Passerelle des Arts is a pedestrian bridge that replaced Paris's first iron bridge, which had become damaged. Today it's a popular meeting place, particularly for artists, painters and photographers, who often display their work there. The Passerelle Simone-de-Beauvoir is the newest pedestrian bridge. It's in Bercy and connects the Bibliothèque Nationale de France to Bercy Park (SEE PaGE 106). The bridge is lens-shaped and spans across the entire width of the river without any supports, other than at each end. It might well be the coolest bridge in the city!

cool, yEaH?

The Pont Alexandre III was named after the Russian Tsar Alexandre III and in the name of Franco-Russian friendship.

The Pont-Neuf has two bridge spans, one on each side of the Île de la Cité, and a total of twelve arches.

43

cool, yEAH?

The original Carnavalet mansion was designed by the same architects that designed the Louvre. You may notice some similarities.

The Carnavalet was the first museum in the world to create period rooms to exhibit art and all sorts of household objects from different places and periods. Nowadays, a lot of museums do it, all over the world... but it all started here!

two hotels turned museums

A long time ago, rich families built mansions in and around Paris, called *hôtels*. Many of them, like the Carnavalet, were eventually converted into museums. The Carnavalet had many owners, including the widow of Francois de Kernevenoy. This name, which somehow became 'Carnavalet', has been associated with the mansion ever since. In 1866, the city bought it and transformed it into a museum focusing on the history of Paris. Here, you'll find scale models that show events like the French Revolution and the crowning of Napoléon I. It's also got recreations of shops and typical rooms from different eras. One of the coolest is the Salle des Enseignes (Signs Room) which has shopkeepers' signs from all over Paris, and from every era. The most famous items, however, are the 4,000-year-old wooden canoes that were used by fisherman on the River Seine. You also shouldn't miss the room full of objects that belonged to kids hundreds of years ago! If you like it, ask your parents to enroll you in one of the many activities and workshops for kids. Or, if you're all curious for more, get a leaflet for one of the self-guided tours around the ancient neighbourhood of Marais. Booklets with quizzes and games for kids are also available with every exhibition. Ask on admission.

Another mansion-turned-museum was the private home of Nélie Jacquemart and Edouard André. The two were avid art collectors who travelled to Italy every year to bring back works of art. The couple created their own museum in their home, which was eventually donated to the Institut de France. It opened to the public in 1913 and has superb rooms and the most amazing grand staircase, that will make you feel like a prince(ss). The museum has a full program of activities for kids, so don't miss out on the opportunity of enjoying some!

cool, yEah?

Notre Dame Cathedral was built with limestone from the quarries that were once where the Catacombs are.

The Catacombs were used as a secret headquarters of the French resistance fighters during World War II.

46

don't bE scaREd! it's oNly a MERE 6 miilioN SKElEtoNs!!!

If you're scared of skeletons and dread the dark, you might want to skip this one. The Catacombs of Paris are easily one of the creepiest places you're likely to visit.

Almost 2,000 years ago, in Roman times, great buildings, monuments, roads and bridges were built in the city that would one day become Paris. To make all this stuff, the Romans mined limestone from quarries. The quarries were used for hundreds of years. During that time, the city also grew, coming closer to the quarries and eventually moving right on top of them! The extra weight caused the quarry tunnels to collapse. You can still visit some of the tunnels that are left, but that's not the creepy part. What's creepy is what's in the tunnels. As the city grew, ten centuries of human remains at the Cemetière des Innocents (Cemetery of the Innocents) were becoming a source of infection for the residents in the area. It was decided that all the skeletons from older Paris cemeteries would be put in these old quarries, where they still are today. Make your way through the tunnels stacked floor to ceiling with bones and skulls, 20 metres below ground! It's like the creepiest Hallowe'en ever.

a cRazy-looKiNG buildiNG packEd witH modERN aRt aNd a lot of utility pipEs!

The Centre Pompidou is a few decades old. That might seem ancient to you, but compared to most Paris museums it's practically a baby! Still, it's one of the most important museums in the city (and the world) because it has the biggest modern and contemporary art collection in all of Europe! It's also one of the craziest looking buildings you'll see in Paris. When it was built, the architects wanted to leave as much space as possible for the artwork inside, so they put all of the technical stuff (like pipes for water, and cables for electricity) on the outside. Even the escalators are on the outside of the building. As you ride up, you'll find yourself inside a plastic tube… just like a hamster!

The centre has many attractions, including the museum, a children's gallery, an institute for music and acoustic research and co-ordination, a library, concert halls, movie theatres and workshops. Spend some time hanging out in the busy square, where you're sure to see mimes, street artists, musicians and entertainers all day long. There's even art outside! The fountain has tons of interesting, weird and colourful sculptures by a famous artist called Niki de Saint-Phalle. (They seem to come all the way from La-La Land!)

cool, yEaH?

The museum's inside-out technical system is colour-coded: blue for air, green for fluid, yellow for electricity, and red for movement and flow (like elevators).

Because of its Beaubourg-Rambuteau location, Parisians sometimes call the Centre Pompidou just 'Beaubourg'.

walk up and down the most beautiful avenue in the world

The Avenue des Champs-Élysées is the most famous and prestigious avenue in Paris—maybe even in the world. And it was the idea of an Italian! The area was filled with fields and gardens until Marie de' Medici decided to create a path to the Tuileries Garden that Catherine de Médicis had built several years before. At first, it was just an avenue of trees, but when André Le Nôtre redesigned the Tuileries Garden, he included the avenue in the plan. Over time, the Champs-Élysées was extended, reaching the l'Étoile, where the Arc de Triomphe now stands. Sidewalks, gas lamps and fountains were installed, followed by the Paris Métro line 1. Because of the avenue's size and location, many parades and royal processions have taken place there. Today it's lined with hundreds of shops, restaurants, hotels and offices and has the reputation for great shopping. It's also the best place in Paris to people-watch!

cool, yEaH?

Renting a small space to open a store here can cost as much as $1.5 million a year!

Today, you'll find stores like Adidas, Benetton, the Disney Store, Nike, Zara, Cartier, the Gap and Sephora along the Champs-Élysées.

cool, yEah?

Also important groups of immigrants in France include: Vietnamese, Cambodian, Senegalese, Hungarian and Polish. Many others come from former colonies or French-speaking countries around the world.

As of January 2008, 64,473,140 people live in France. Of those, about 4.9 million are foreign-born immigrants (that's 8% of the country's population).

a city of many cultures

Like many European countries, France owes a lot of its cultural richness to immigrants—people who originally came from other countries. In fact, Paris is one of the world's most multicultural cities! The largest groups are Portuguese, Spanish, Italian, Romanian, Russian and Ukrainian. Unfortunately, people sometimes treat immigrants unfairly, forgetting that they helped to build the country, and not taking into consideration how brave a person has to be to leave behind their country, their family, and everything they know and love.

The Cité Nationale de l'Histoire de l'Immigration is one of Paris's newest museums, on the edges of the Bois de Vincennes (SEE page 40), and it aims to teach people about the importance of immigration in France. You'll find the museum inside the Palais de la Porte Dorée (Palace of the Golden Door), which was built for the 1931 Colonial Exhibition. The building uses the art nouveau style and is gorgeous inside and outside. For many years it was a museum of African and Oceanic arts, until Quai Branly opened (SEE page 26). Today only the tropical aquarium and the beautiful, grand ground floor rooms are open to the public.

Upstairs, the Immigration Museum's exhibition is fully interactive. You'll learn about why people leave their countries, what their living conditions are like in France, and how diverse the country has become because of immigration. You'll also learn how people travelled, cooked and what they did for entertainment back in their home countries. There's even a special section of display cases that tell the personal stories of older people who came to France. You can hear their own words with the audio tour, and look at the special items in their lives behind the glass.

Puzzling Musical Instruments

Have you ever heard a metallophone, an octobass or a pluriarc? If you're into music, there's a wealth of weird and wonderful instruments for you to discover at Cité de la Musique. The goal of this place—which is part museum, part school and part concert hall—is to introduce people to musical instruments and the culture around them. They've got an impressive collection of instruments, works of art and scale models going as far back as 400 years, and coming from all over the world. This is just the place to find out what a pluriarc is, what a tortoise-guitar looks like, or to check out the octobass—an instrument so big that two people are needed to play it.

If you've got a talent for making music, the gamelan workshop is just the thing. Not only will you learn to play an instrument, you'll get to play with an entire orchestra! A gamelan is a set of instruments from Java Island in Indonesia that usually includes metallophones, xylophones, drums and lots of gongs. But if you'd rather just sit back and listen, then attend a concert or musical show. And don't even worry if classical music isn't your thing. The Cité's programming includes pretty much every type of music in the book! Soon it will also be the home of the Paris Philharmonic Orchestra.

cool, yEaH?

There are over 4,000 instruments from all over the world in the museum's collection.

Only three octobasses were ever made! Today, only two of them still exist somewhere.

cool, yEah?

La Géode's hemispherical screen is 1,000 square metres, or 10 times bigger than in a normal movie theatre.

You thought the Centre Pompidou (SEE paGE 48) was big? The Cité has enough room for four Pompidous!

tHE biggEst sciENcE musEum iN tHE wHolE of EuRopE!

Cité des Sciences et de l'Industrie isn't the only science museum in the city, but it is the most modern. You'll find it in the Parc de la Villette, standing on its own 'island', surrounded by a moat! Inside is the Cité des Enfants, a science museum designed specifically for kids.

When you visit, you'll learn about many areas of science and technology, including cars, energy, math, light, sound, humans, outer space and astronomy, health, plants, nature, agriculture… the list goes on and on. And those are just the permanent exhibits. Like any science museum, there are also tons of hands-on experiments to try. And be sure not to miss the shows at the planetarium, the Géode (an IMAX theatre inside a perfect sphere) and the cool Cinaxe (a simulator where the room moves with the action on the screen to give you a virtual trip). You can see pictures of La Géode in the Parc de la Villette (SEE pagE 104)... and after that, you'll want your picture taken with it!

a placE foR KiNGs aNd cRowNs

The Île-de-la-Cité, where you'll find the Conciergerie & Sainte-Chapelle, was the original seat of power for the first French kings. The Conciergerie was where the king met with his council and government. Sainte-Chapelle was built in the 13th century, after King Louis IX bought a relic that he treasured more than anything else: something that was believed to be Jesus Christ's Crown of Thorns. Such an important item naturally needed a really fancy home, and so the King ordered Sainte-Chapelle to be built for the crown. The building is made up of two separate chapels: the upper chapel, which houses the relics and the lower chapel, which was used by the palace staff.

The upper chapel was richly decorated and still contains 15 stained glass windows with 1,113 scenes telling the biblical story of mankind from Genesis to Christ's resurrection. These windows should be looked at from left to right, and from the bottom up. When he took over power, Saint-Louis's grandson, King Philippe IV expanded the Conciergerie and built one of the most impressive palaces of the Middle Ages. One of the towers of the Conciergerie is the Tour de l'Horloge (Clock Tower), which boasted the first public clock in Paris. At one point, the lower floor housed the palace soldiers and their horses, like a stinky underground village!

cool, yEaH?

The Crown of Thorns cost the king 135,000 livres. But the Sainte-Chapelle only cost 40,000 livres to build!

The word concierge comes from 'comte des cierges' (keeper of the candles). This was the person in charge of lighting candles in castles! Over time, he also became responsible for opening and closing doors, and keeping all the keys safe together!

A century later, after the assassination of royal advisors, the French King moved to the Louvre and Château de Vincennes, which offered better protection. The King's *concierge* was left in charge of the entire place. During the French Revolution, parliament also moved out of the building, leaving only the courts and a prison, which held many prisoners, notably *gens de qualité* ('people of quality' or people of noble blood). The best of all was Marie-Antoinette, King Louis XVI's wife! She was kept here for several months, while her supporters made some failed attempts to free her. The only thing they achieved was to have two *gendarmes* placed *inside* of the cell. One of them had to have his eyes on her, 24/7!

two tributes to the fine arts

Paris has hosted the Universal Exposition (World Fair) several times. The one in 1900 celebrated the achievements of the past century while welcoming the next. Every time the city hosts an Expo, they try to out-do the last one by building newer, bigger or better buildings for it… and it gets harder every time! The Eiffel tower had been built for the 1889 Expo, so that was hard to beat, to say the least.

City officials began working on the challenge almost immediately. What they decided to build, in the end, was a palace for the fine arts. A competition was held to design and build it, and in the end, several entries were used to create the large glass exhibition hall called the Grand Palais, where the Palais de la Découverte (SEE PaGE 98) is located today. But it still wasn't enough! Instead of one, the city built two palaces. The second is called Petit Palais. It's similar to the Grand Palais, except that the dome looks more like it was inspired by Les Invalides. Today it's home to the City of Paris Museum of Fine Arts (Musée des Beaux-Arts de la Ville de Paris) and displays art and artifacts from ancient Egypt to 1900. They both look great at sunset on the riverbank!

cool, yEah?

The 1900 Summer Olympics (the 2nd Olympic Games of the modern age) were held as part of the 1900 Expo.

Many technological advances and inventions made their debuts at the 1900 Expo: talking films, escalators and diesel engines that ran on peanut oil!

what's New is old again...

In 1246, when Paris officially became a city, the first alderman (something like a mayor) was chosen as a representative to the king. But it wasn't until the 14th century, when the House of Pillars near the Place de Grève was turned into a city hall, that the city's government had a home. The building wasn't the greatest though, and because a city like Paris needed an appropriate city hall, King François I ordered a new building to be built in 1533. Except, nobody was in a hurry to get it done! It took a whopping 100 years to build the new city hall, and poor King François died long before he could see it completed!

During the Franco-Prussian War in 1871 revolutionaries set the new building on fire, also destroying all the city archives. A competition to build another city hall was held and officials actually voted for a plan based on the original style! So today, even though the building isn't even 150 years old, it looks way older. Paris city hall is still based here. There's also a small space where exhibitions are held while the square is used for outdoor events, like ice-skating during the winter, large concerts, Christmas markets, carousels and more!

cool, yEah?

The square's name dates to 1830.

An underground tunnel connects l'Hôtel de Ville with nearby army barracks (for security).

HotEl dE villE (city hall)
Hôtel de Ville

a woRKShop that was callEd HotEl to luRE soldiERs in

In 1670, King Louis XVIII decided to make a building to house disabled soldiers, or those who were too old to serve in his armies. The complex was home to about 4,000 soldiers. It wasn't like a spa, a hotel or a nursing home though. Far from it! The men living there had to work, making uniforms, shoes, tapestries and doing book illumination (painting the pictures in ancient books). Today, Les Invalides contains museums and monuments relating to France's military history, a hospital, a retirement home for war veterans and a burial site. But it's most famous for being the last resting place of Napoléon Bonaparte—a French military and political leader who had a big impact on the history of Europe.

Under Napoléon's command, the French army became one of the strongest in European history. He led his armies against every major European country, winning many victories. Eventually, he was defeated after a failed invasion of Russia and died in exile. He was first buried on St. Helena (an island in the middle of the South Atlantic), but King Louis-Philippe got permission to return Napoléon's remains to France many years later. His body was first brought to St. Jerome's Chapel, and upon the building's completion was moved under the dome at Les Invalides.

cool, yEah?

Napoléon sold the French colony of Louisiana to the US to avoid France's bankruptcy. It cost them only $7.40 per square kilometre (3 cents per acre)! What a bargain!

Église du Dôme was the royal chapel and was a copy of St. Peter's Basilica in Rome.

HaNG ouT WiTH tHE RiCH aNd faMouS oN tHEiR quiEt islaNd

If you're looking for some calm amid the busy pace of Paris life, head to Île Saint-Louis. This natural island has narrow streets, no Métro stations and only two bus stops. It's also got some seriously stylish castle-like houses.

Once, Île Saint-Louis was swampy land, divided into two small islets—one belonged to Notre Dame de Paris (the cathedral) and the other was used for grazing cattle. Nobody lived there until the 1600s, when King Louis XIII approved plans to reconnect the islets and develop them with streets, bridges and houses. The people who moved there were rich, and they built *hôtels particuliers* (private mansions). They were the finest homes designed by the finest architects and decorated by the finest artists. After the reign of Louis XIII, though, the nobility abandoned the island by the truckload, and in the next few centuries it became a shady neighbourhood… until the 1950s, that is, when the island was restored to its former glory.

Walk over one of the five bridges that connect the city of Paris to Île Saint-Louis and check out the small but upscale selection of restaurants, shops, cafés and ice cream parlours. By the time you leave, you'll feel like a million bucks! (And probably shelled out a million for your ice cream.)

cool, yEaH?

The island's layout was designed by Louis Le Vau, who also designed the Château de Versailles.

In French, 'hôtel' can mean different things: a hôtel particulier is a private mansion; a hôtel de dieu is an old religious hospital; hôtel de ville is the city hall; and a hôtel touristique is an actual hotel!

EDITOR'S CHOICE
JETSETTERS

a placE wHERE oNly kids RulE!

Today, major cities are multi-cultural with people from all over the world, but it wasn't always this way. In 1877, Paris had a zoo called l'Acclimatation Anthropologique, but it didn't have animals on display. Instead, it had humans. Parisians, many of whom had never seen any non-Europeans before, were curious about foreigners. Many African people were exhibited in this human zoo, as were Inuits and other Native Americans. At the beginning, the zoo was considered important for scientists and anthropologists (those studying human behaviour), but it wasn't long before anthropologists and the general public realized that human zoos were actually very inhumane! In 1912, the zoo was closed down and later converted to an amusement park.

Today, the Jardin d'Acclimatation in the Bois du Boulogne (SEE PaGE 38), is a big outdoor theme park, and it's all for kids. There's a mini farm, boat and train rides, an aviary, a petting zoo, pony rides, miniature golf, bumper cars, an archery range, a theatre and more. If the weather isn't so great (or even if it is) you might also want to check out the two museums on-site: a children's art museum (the Musée en Herbe), and the Musée National des Arts et Traditions Populaires.

cool, yEaH?

Although the Bois de Boulogne is a lovely place to walk around and have fun, it sure wasn't always like this!
During the Hundred Years War, the Bois was a favourite hangout for terrorizing forest bandits.

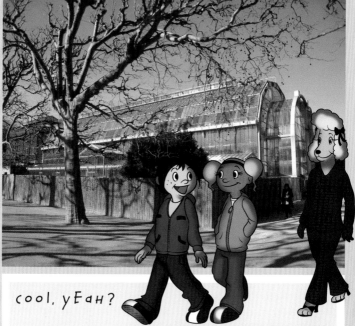

cool, yEaH?

La Ménagerie is one of the oldest public zoos in the whole world.

The garden has a False Acacia (Black Locust) tree that was planted in 1636. It is believed to be the oldest tree in Paris.

plants, plants and plenty more plants!

Sure, plants are leafy and green and nice to look at, but did you know that they're also great for healing? Plants have been used as medicine for a long, long time— longer than medicine, as we know it today, has been around! The first records of plants and herbs being used to treat sickness were shown in cave paintings discovered in France that date back to 13,000–25,000 BC! In the Middle Ages, when kings and queens were sick, they used herbs prescribed by their doctors.

Back then, the Jardin des Plantes was a private royal garden of medicinal plants planted by King Louis XIII's doctor to serve the King. Shortly after, it was opened to the public for visits. Over the years, it was transformed from a medicinal herb garden to a botanical garden. Today, the garden has thousands of plants and is also the home to the National Museum of Natural History (SEE PaGE 90), a botanical school, a rose garden, a maze (the Labyrinth) and La Ménagerie. La Ménagerie is a small zoo that was once located at the Château de Versailles. So here's your chance to bow to some royal lions, giraffes, monkeys, birds, snakes and more.

a little latin, a lot of learning

Can you imagine if you had to take every subject at school in Latin? Back in 1217, when La Sorbonne—a famous Paris university—was opened, Latin was the language of learning, the language of church and even the language ambassadors from different kingdoms used to communicate with each other. It's why the area around the university became known as the Quartier Latin, or Latin Quarter.

La Sorbonne is only one of the many schools in the area. It was originally a theological (religious) centre, but was closed during the French Revolution like all religious institutions, and was later reopened by Napoléon I. Schools aren't the only things you can see in this area, either. While you're there, check out the Panthéon (SEE PAGE 102), the Museum of the Middle Ages (SEE PAGE 92), the National Museum of Natural History (SEE PAGE 90) and the Arab World Institute, down by the river Seine (SEE PAGE 32). Today, the Latin Quarter is known for its lively atmosphere, its artists, its intellectuals and its relaxed, unconventional way of life. This is partly because of the students who live there and hang out around the beautiful, café-packed Boulevard Saint Michel, or have their baguettes in the Luxembourg Garden (SEE PAGE 74).

cool, yEaH?

In Roman times, Paris (then called Lutetia) was a walled city located in today's Latin Quarter.

Many languages inherited most of their words from Latin. Take French, Italian, Spanish, Portuguese, and Romanian, for example. But almost every European language includes lots of Latin words in its vocabulary.

pONiES, toy boats, baGuETtES, bEES, aNd MUCH MoRE!

The Jardin du Luxembourg is a great place to play outside. You'll find this beautiful public garden beside the Palais du Luxembourg. Sail toy boats in the octagonal pond, learn all about bees and beekeeping in the garden's apiary (bee yard), ride ponies, play tennis, take a whirl on the merry-go-round or watch the famous puppet shows of Marionettes du Luxembourg. Whatever you do, though, don't walk on the grass or ride a bicycle!! Both of these things are strictly forbidden.

Make sure you stop and have a look at the palace, too, before you go. It's similar to architecture you'd see in Florence. This is because several of France's queens were from the powerful Medici family, the rulers of Florence (now part of Italy). Marie de' Medici, who was responsible for transforming the Champs-Élysées, also built the Palais du Luxembourg. She grew up in Florence and wanted something to remind her of her home. The garden, on the other hand, is much more a Paris-style garden, with a large pond (the Grand Bassin), terraces, lawns, flowers, alleys, an orchard and many statues. The palace was a royal residence until the French Revolution. Today it houses the French Senate. Other than Senators walking around the park, you will notice couples on their lunch break, people doing sports and eating huge baguettes bought in Boulevard Saint Michel. Some people say this is the most beautiful park in the world.

cool, yEaH?

During the French Revolution, the palace was first a factory and then a prison.

The first model of the Statue of Liberty is in this park.

74

tHE oNE muSEum tHat's SuRE to maKE aN imPRESSioN!

The Musée d'Orsay contains work by some of the world's most famous artists—like Cézanne, Dégas, Pissaro and van Gogh—but it's most well-known for its big collection of Impressionist paintings. These are paintings of ordinary subject matter, where you can see the brush strokes, where there are weird visual angles and where there's usually some movement taking place. See if you can spot paintings of this style as you walk through the museum.

The Musée d'Orsay wasn't always a museum. It was once the first electric railway station, and was considered to be one of the most beautiful. But trains soon became too long to fit in the station, and it had to be closed. Over the years, the abandoned station was used for different things. During World War II, it was a reception centre for returning, liberated prisoners. At one time, it was even used as a parking lot! It was almost demolished, but was saved by President Georges Pompidou. The French government then decided to convert the station into the museum you see today, which is focused on 19th and 20th century art and contains paintings, sculptures, engravings, photos, film, architecture and decorative arts.

cool, yEaH?

More metal was used to construct the Gare d'Orsay than for the Eiffel Tower.

The original station also had a hotel in it, but it's now long gone.

77

youR famouS (waX) buddiEs

Where can you meet Céline Dion, Ghandi and Louis XIV (the longest ruling King of France) all under one roof? Well, if you don't mind the fact that they look a little waxy, at the Grévin Museum. The museum opened way back in the late 19th century. Photography was uncommon then, and TV didn't exist. The public wanted to see the people they were reading about in the newspaper, and this was the inspiration for the Musée Grévin—where life-sized wax figures were created of the people who were making headlines.

To make a wax figure, first the sculptor meets the person and makes a clay version of their head. They find out the exact colour of the person's eyes, hair and skin. The clay head is then used to make a mold. For the body, a look-alike is used to make a plaster mold. Beeswax is poured into the head mold, while resin is poured into the body mold. The finished shape is sanded to remove any seams. Details come next— eyes, teeth, hair, eyebrows. Make-up (which is actually paint) follows. You can learn more about the process during your visit. Then find your favourite celebrity and have your picture taken with them like you're old buddies!

cool, yEaH?

The wax figures have real human hair—about 500,000 hairs per figure, all attached one by one!

The Académie Grévin, made up of at least 11 people who are usually journalists, elect people to be included in the museum. Between four and six celebrities are added each year.

tHESE sculptuRES look so REal. it's EvEN kind of scaRy...

Have you ever seen a sculpture that seemed so real, you had to look twice to make sure it wasn't about to move? Auguste Rodin was a French artist who was best known for exactly this type of artwork. He included all the details and imperfections. If his model had a broken nose, for example, so did his sculpture. Rodin's first full-size work, l'Age d'airain (The Age of Bronze) was so realistic that people thought his mold was made directly from the model. At the Rodin Museum, you'll see some of the artist's best-known works.

The museum is in the Hôtel Biron—the same private mansion Rodin once rented rooms in to use as his studio. At the same time, the building was also home to many artists, including Henri Matisse. Before he died, Rodin gave all his work, and everything he collected (including work by Matisse, Monet and van Gogh) to the state with the condition that a museum be created for his work at the Hôtel Biron. As you walk around his sculptures, inside and in the gardens, try to pick out the one that looks the most real to you. Some may even look like your mom or your uncle!

cool, yEah?

The original molds for Rodin's sculptures are at his home in Meudon.

Rodin never finished The Gates of Hell. The bronze sculpture was cast after his death. The first three versions are in Philadelphia, Paris and Tokyo.

"HouStoN CalliNG jEtSEttERS-1: pREpaRE FoR takEoff!"

If you're into airplanes, don't forget to fly by the Musée de l'Air et de l'Espace (Museum of Air and Space). You'll learn all about air travel over the past few hundred years. And for anyone more interested in space, the planetarium provides a great, close-up view. Try to catch an exciting session!

The museum's exhibits highlight France's influence in the field of aviation and also showcase some of the strange contraptions people built over the years, trying to fly! You'll also see gliders, balloons, war planes, jets, rockets and even some prototypes. One highlight is the special exhibition about Antoine (Jean-Baptiste Marie Roger) de Saint Exupéry, the most famous French pilot of all time. He is also the author and illustrator of *Le Petit Prince* (*The Little Prince*), one of the most famous books in the world! Worth checking out and getting your own copy of the book! But the coolest piece in the museum is the Concorde 001, which is on display next to the last Concorde airplane that flew a round-trip from Paris to New York, back in 2003. A Concorde accident eventually convinced airlines to ground this type of airplane forever due to a technical glitch that could not be solved. But for a while, it was the fastest aircraft in the world.

The museum is right at the edge of France's first airport, (Le Bourget). In 1927 it became famous when Charles Lindbergh landed his Spirit of St. Louis there, becoming the first person to complete a solo non-stop transatlantic flight. Two weeks before this, Le Bourget was the departure point for two French pilots who attempted a transatlantic flight (Charles Nungesser and François Coli) in their plane, l'Oiseau Blanc (The White Bird). The plane and pilots mysteriously disappeared somewhere over the Atlantic Ocean, and the museum now has the only remaining piece of The White Bird: its landing gear.

cool, yEah?

The Concorde was so fast that you could arrive in New York before you even left Paris! (So to speak). That was possible because the supersonic flight took only 4 ½ hours, but New York's time zone is 6 hours behind Paris's. Therefore, if you left Paris at 8 pm you'd be in New York at 6:30 pm, that is one hour and a half before you actually left!!!

cool, yEah?

The museum has a special audio-guide just for kids.

The complex was originally fortified around its entire perimeter. You can still see sections of the wall today.

calling all junioR inVENtoRs

If you come to this museum expecting to see stuff made out of pipe cleaners, construction paper and glue, you'll be in for a big surprise! The museum actually showcases original instruments, machines, models, drawings and plans in seven categories: scientific instruments, materials, construction, communication, energy, mechanics and transportation. It should really be called the *Museum of Inventions* or *the Museum of Technology,* not the Museum of Arts and Crafts! When you visit, you can see one of the earliest airplanes ever designed, as well as Foucault's pendulum—an early experiment to demonstrate the rotation of the Earth.

The building dates all the way back to the 11th century when it used to be a priory (a house where monks and nuns lived). During the French Revolution in the 18th century, when most religious buildings were confiscated and sold, the building was given to the Conservatoire National des Arts et Métiers (National Conservatory of Arts and Crafts). Its new role was to improve France's industries through new inventions. The museum was almost like a catalogue back then, where French technology was displayed for future investors to browse through. Today it's also a school and a research organization.

85

lEaRN all abouT HaNuKKaH, sHabbaT, RosH HasHaNaH aNd otHER sTRaNGE HEbREW woRds

This museum presents the art and history of Jews living in France, as well as the history of Judaism as a whole. When you walk through, you'll see artifacts, art, furniture, textiles, manuscripts and films that tell the story of this group's often-difficult history.

Today's France has the largest Jewish population in all of Europe, but Jewish people weren't always made to feel welcome in the past. In fact, they were forced out of France several times. After the French Revolution, Jews were made full citizens for the first time. Still, like other religious buildings and churches, Jewish synagogues and organizations were closed down or destroyed during the Reign of Terror, a violent time during the revolution.

Another big push for equality came from Napoléon I, who made Judaism an official religion in France along with Roman Catholicism and Protestantism. Many Jews returned to France after the revolution. In Paris, they resettled in the Marais district—an area that had been a big Jewish neighbourhood hundreds of years before. Jews soon became very involved in theatre, politics, literature, philosophy and art in France. Jewish artists, like Modigliani, Chagall and Soutine, became famous in the early 1900s and highlight the role Jews played in 20th century art.

cool, yEaH?

Hôtel de Saint-Aignan, the museum's building, dates back to 1650. During the 20th century, before it became a museum, many Jewish people lived there.

cool, yEaH?

David Copperfield once made the Statue of Liberty SEEM to disappear. (It was an illusion.)

Harry Houdini was inspired by a famous French magician, Jean Eugène Robert-Houdin, who is often considered to be the first modern magician, and one of the most illusive of all times!

COME aS a Kid,
lEavE aS a coNJuRoR

If you've got a trick or two up your sleeve, this is the place for you. At Musée de la Magie, not only will you see a magic show, you'll also learn how many of the tricks are done. But, be warned—magicians guard their secrets carefully! So when it comes to learning how that rabbit really comes out of that hat, what's said in this museum, stays in this museum.

You'll learn about production (making something from nothing, like that rabbit we mentioned), vanishing (making something disappear, often a coin), transformation (making something change forms), restoration (destroying something and then restoring it), teleportation (moving something from one place to another), escapology (escaping from a restraining device), levitation (making something float), penetration (making something solid like a sword pass through another object, like your body!) and prediction (predicting a choice or occurrence, for example with a deck of cards). Your visit includes a short illusionism show in which you may find yourself on stage. It also includes an exhibition of some of the weirdest contraptions that magicians have been using throughout time. You'll be a bit of a Harry Houdini by the time you leave...

89

so much biodiversity that your mind will be blown away!

If you're always bugging your parents to walk instead of drive, and reminding them to reduce, reuse and recycle, you'll want to visit The Muséum National d'Histoire Naturelle.

The museum is made up of several different buildings and gardens, including a zoo, but the most impressive gallery is the Grande Galerie de l'Évolution (Grand Gallery of Evolution). Here, life-sized animal and sea life displays, interactive displays, light shows and sounds all come together to point out the importance of the earth's biodiversity and the protection that it needs. They also explain Charles Darwin's Theory of Evolution in a really cool way. Stop by to understand the role that humans have played in evolution, how we have changed, and how we continue to change life on earth.

The museum, as it stands today, dates back to the French Revolution, but the site's history goes back a lot further, like most things in Paris. At one time, it was the Jardin Royal des Plantes Médicinales (Royal Garden of Medicinal Herbs) and was used by the royal doctors to get the herbal medicines they needed to keep the king healthy.

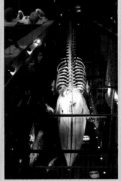

cool, yEah?

Uranium's radioactive properties were discovered at the museum by a scientist named Henri Becquerel. He received the Nobel Prize for it.

There are about 68 million specimens in the museum's collection.

bE amazEd by mEdiEval aRt

In the 19th century, an art collector named Alexandre Du Sommerard, moved into this building (then called Hôtel de Cluny) where he was able to display his large collection of objects and art from the Middle Ages. After his death, the castle became the Musée National du Moyen Âge. The museum has stained-glass windows, sculptures, armour, costumes, jewellery, décor and tapestries. The highlight of the museum is *La dame à la licorne* (*The Lady and the Unicorn*), a series of six huge tapestries hanging from the walls of a dark, moon-shaped room.

Five of them represent the five human senses—sight, hearing, taste, smell and touch. The sixth, titled *À mon seul désir* (to my only desire) is a bit of a mystery, and everyone seems to have an opinion about it. Check it out. Keep your eyes open and you'll see a plaque commemorating Nicolas Flamel. Any Harry Potter fan will remember him from *Harry Potter and the Philosopher's Stone* (called *Harry Potter and the Sorcerer's Stone* in some countries). If you can't find it, just ask the staff. Outside, a medieval-style garden showcases the nine medicinal plants used in the Middle Ages… it's nothing like our pharmacies today!

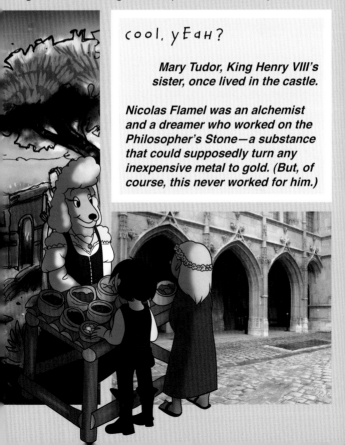

cool, yEah?

Mary Tudor, King Henry VIII's sister, once lived in the castle.

Nicolas Flamel was an alchemist and a dreamer who worked on the Philosopher's Stone—a substance that could supposedly turn any inexpensive metal to gold. (But, of course, this never worked for him.)

a muSEuM you caN RollERbladE youR way tHRougH!

If you're not a big fan of stuffy museums where everything is all historic and fragile; and loud, scary alarms go off if you touch things; and you have to whisper so you don't disturb other people… you might like this one. Along the River Seine you'll find the Musée de la Sculpture en Plein Air (Open Air Sculpture Museum). It's completely outdoors, and completely free. You can touch stuff, and run, and talk as loudly as you want to. You can even rollerblade or ride your bike! Plus, it's just metres away from the water. The cool, risqué-looking sculptures you'll see here are located all along the paths, and you can even pose in front of them if you want to. Most are by extremely famous French and international artists, from the second half of the 20th century (1950-2000). There is one rule, though: as usual in Paris, you have to stay off the grass!

cool, yEaH?

The museum is located in the Jardin Tino Rossi —a garden dedicated to a famous French singer and actor.

Musée de la Sculpture en Plein Air has one of the best riverside views in the city.

MiLES aNd MiLES of MuSEuM(S)

If you like museums, look no further. The Palais de Chaillot is like a one-stop museum shop! It is home to the Cité de l'Architecture et du Patrimoine, the Musée National des Monuments Français, the Musée National de la Marine and the Musée de l'Homme.

During the Spanish Civil War, 1820–1823, the French king, Louis XVIII, sent his forces into Spain where they captured the Fort of Trocadéro near the southern city of Cádiz. This helped restore King Ferdinand as the ruling king of Spain. The battle was so important to the French that they named an area of Paris 'place du Trocadéro', and this is where Chaillot Palace is today.

In 1889, the Aquarium du Trocadéro (now Cinéaqua—SEE PaGE 18) was built under the palace. The current palace, like many buildings in Paris, was built for the 1937 Expo and the original palace had to be destroyed to put it up. The designers for the new palace had an interesting problem. The Eiffel Tower wasn't far away from the building site, and if the new palace was too small, it would look ridiculous in the tower's shadow. So instead of building something tall to compete with the tower, they decided to build something that stretched out for what seemed like miles.

cool, yEaH?

The name 'Trocadéro' comes from a Spanish word meaning 'a place of trade'.

The quarries in Trocadéro were used to build the aquarium. Other quarries in the city were used for the solidification work in the Catacombs.

pIEasE do n̶o̶t touch ~~EVERY~~thing

You won't find exhibits stashed away behind Plexiglas here. At Palais de la Découverte, getting right up close to the exhibits and touching them is part of the experience, and everything is hands-on and interactive. The staff is always conducting live experiments that reveal science as it actually happens. And if you're interested in astronomy, there's a planetarium where you can discover the stars and planets. There's even a room dedicated to the Sun!

In the 1920s and 1930s, most people knew very little about astronomy, biology, chemistry, physics and mathematics. The International Exhibition on Arts and Techniques in Modern Life was held to show the general public a glimpse of the progress being made in science. The organizer was a man named Jean Perrin, who won the Nobel Prize for Physics in 1926 for his work on the atom. The exhibition was a huge hit and, in 1937, the Palais de la Découverte was opened as a permanent museum to promote and popularize science.

cool, yEaн?

Staff at the Palais de la Découverte conduct more than 40 science demonstrations each day!

The museum has an actual piece of moon rock brought back by Apollo 11 in 1969. It was a gift from the United States.

cool, yEah?

The palace was once home to the Queen of England, who had been exiled during the English Civil War.

Cardinal Richelieu was the main villain in Alexandre Dumas's novel The Three Musketeers!

Do you see the 260 black and white striped columns in the Cour d'Honneur? They're a work of art by Daniel Buren called 'Les Deux Plateaux' (The Two Plateaus).

EN GaRdE, caRdiNal...

The Palais Royal didn't start out as a royal palace. It was Cardinal Richelieu, King Louis XIII's all-powerful First Minister, who had it built, and it was known as Palais Cardinal. When the cardinal died in 1642, he left it to Louis XIII and that's when it became Palais Royal. King Louis XIV, who later built Les Invalides, Place Vendôme and Château de Versailles, grew up there.

The building has changed a lot over the years. Today it looks nothing like the original palace, and no royalty lives there. Instead, it's home to the Ministry of Culture and the Constitutional Council. Even though the building isn't open to visitors, the Cour d'Honneur (Courtyard of Honour) and the Jardin du Palais Royal are. The garden centres around a fountain and is surrounded by restaurants, shops and galleries.

101

a vERy classy cRypt

Sure, as honours go, it might not seem as cool as a giant trophy, or as fun as that pizza party your class got for collecting the most pledges in the charity run... but anyone who gets buried at the Panthéon after they die can at least rest easy, knowing that their accomplishments will go down in history! The building, which was originally a church called Église Sainte-Geneviève (Church of Saint Geneviève), is now a final resting place of honour for some of France's most notable citizens.

In 1774, King Louis XV vowed to replace the ruined original church if he recovered from an illness. He did, but the construction took more than 40 years. By then, the French Revolution had begun. And that was a time when the monarchy and the Roman Catholic Church were very unpopular... Many churches were destroyed, but Sainte-Geneviève was spared and rededicated as a *pantheon*, which means a temple dedicated to *all* the Gods.

The national heroes buried there include artists, writers, scientists and anyone else that helped make France the powerful republic that it is today. Some of the most famous people include Pierre and Marie Curie (scientists that won the Noble Prize), Voltaire (writer and philosopher), Louis Braille (inventor of the first alphabet for the blind) and Alexandre Dumas (writer of *The Three Musketeers*).

cool, yEah?

In 1851, physicist Léon Foucault demonstrated the rotation of the Earth by constructing the 67-metre Foucault pendulum beneath the central dome in the Panthéon. You can see the pendulum at the Museum of Arts and Crafts (SEE paGE 84).

There's enough space for 300 people to be buried in the crypt at the Panthéon, but only 74 people have received this honour so far.

cool, yЕaн?

The park is the second-largest green space in Paris. (The largest is the Père-Lachaise Cemetery.)

The submarine Argonaute, docked in la Villette, has been around the world 10 times.

a faNtastic, futuRistic paRk

Can you imagine being so powerful that you could just order people to build you a city? That's what life was like for Napoléon III who, in 1867, decided he wanted a small city to be built where Parc de la Villette is today.

It wasn't your typical city, though. Instead, it was made up of warehouses, meat and livestock markets, and slaughterhouses for cattle. This 'city' stood until 1974 but, in 2000, a decision was made to transform the area into a park, and a competition was held to design the new Parc de la Villette.

The park was designed in a very modern style to include large open spaces, green space, sidewalks, bike trails, bridges, gardens, play areas, fountains, sculptures, rides and merry-go-rounds. The park is also home to the Cité des Sciences et de l'Industrie (City of Science and Industry—SEE PaGE 56), La Géode (an IMAX theatre), Cité de la Musique (City of Music—SEE PaGE 54), Grande Halle de la Villette and the Argonaute (a 1950s submarine open to visitors). The gardens have unique themes: mirrors, things that scare kids (but actually don't!), wind and dunes, acrobatics, balancing acts, climbing, bamboo and shade. It's so much fun you can't even handle it!

blossoms, winding paths, books and a really cool bridge...

Bercy used to be made up of wineries and vineyards, integrated in the Bois de Vincennes. Today, it's got flowerbeds all over the place, arranged in traditional French garden styles (like the rose garden, the labyrinth, the fragrant garden or the kitchen garden). But there are also reminders of the past, like vines and century-old trees preserved from the original woods. Another section of the park, called the romantic garden, features ruins, fake mountains, a canal and birch trees—it looks almost like a painting. The two sides of the park are linked by cool arch bridges. In one end you'll see some metal statues and the weirdest bridge ever, 106 undulating meters across the river toward the four skyscrapers on the other side: the National Library of France. The library is also called Bibliothèque François Mitterrand (like the nearest subway station), in honour of a late president of France. Get yourself a baguette and eat it on the majestic riverside steps, overlooking the sunken gardens and Paris's skyline. At lunchtime, you'll see hundreds of smart-looking people coming out to do the same. And you could also catch a movie in the huge Cinemax next door!

cool, yeah?

The National Library of France – François Mitterrand has 10 million books, and growing. That's a lot of books!

The Passerelle Simone-de-Beauvoir was named like this in honour of a great French writer, and it was fabricated in the Eiffel factories (just like the Eiffel Tower!)

Parc de Bercy used to be part of the royal hunting grounds of Vincennes. Only the king and his guests (or people authorized by the king) could hunt there.

Once you are in the area, make a stop at Bercy Village, a shopping mall built in an old Parisian village. The shopping here is unique (as are the shops), and there are loads of activities for kids, especially on weekends. You'll love it and your parents will, too. Besides, you'll need every excuse you can get to ride that awesome driver-less Métro again— it is controlled by a remote computer, so get the front seat for a maddening thrill of a ride!

cool, yEah?

From the Grande Arche, you can get to Quatre Temps shopping mall. When it was built, it was the largest shopping centre in Europe. It's still pretty massive.

La Défense is Europe's biggest business district.

sHiNy, tall officE toWERs aNd aN officE aRcH as wEll!

Paris is a beautiful city, full of historic buildings and great architecture and, let's face it, office towers and high rises can be kind of ugly looking. That's why La Défense was created. In the 1960s, it was decided that large office buildings should be kept together in one spot, so they wouldn't change the look and feel of Paris's older neighbourhoods. That seems to have been a really smart and popular decision. Today you can see the spiked, shiny skyline of La Défense from high points like the Arc de Triomphe.

La Défense is also the site of the Grande Arche, one of Paris's most modern and imposing landmarks, and a modern take on the Arc de Triomphe, just down the avenue. Make sure you stop by and ride up the elevator. You'll be rewarded with a great view of the city. You'll find the Grande Arche at the west end of the grand axis formed by the Champs-Élysées, the Place de la Concorde and the Arc de Triomphe. Oh, and here's a photo-tip: the sunlight reflected in the mirrored buildings makes for great shots, especially at sunset!

HOW PARIS BECAME, WELL...PARIS!

Paris Story is a great place to start your visit. You'll learn about the history of Paris, and find out all it has to offer visitors today. The one-hour film shown there combines videos, photos, documents and music to tell the (hi)story of Paris in a fun way, going through its music, fashion, architecture, politics and economy over the years. Next to the main screen there is a holographic poet that goes on and on about the beauty of this city... it looks like he is in the room!

Paris is a huge city with tons of interesting buildings and places to see—but you'd need weeks, or even months, to get to them all. That's why Paris Miniature, a gigantic interactive model of the city, is so great for visitors. You can use it like a huge 3-D map to see all of the most popular and important buildings, monuments, streets, parks, fortified walls and more! The bird's eye view will give you an idea of where everything is, what's close to what and how to make the most of your visit instead of spending hours in the Métro every day. The model also shows a few places outside Paris as well as attractions you might not even find in a travel guide—even this one! Over 100 monuments are marked on the map by their actual miniatures, and a series of buttons allows you to illuminate routes and places for better reference. One 1/2 hour spent in Paris Story will make your visit to Paris a bliss!

cool, yEah?

Back in the Roman times, Paris was called Lutetia (Lutèce in French). Although there aren't many ruins left, some are still there. Ask where!

The history of the place we nowadays call Paris goes back 2,000 years!

JUNIOR EDITOR'S CHOICE JETSETTERS

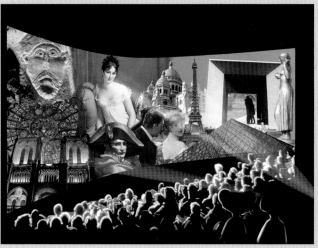

aVENUE UPON aVENUE of dEad VIPS (vERy intElligEnt pEoplE)

Visiting a cemetery might not be on your 'top-ten list of fun stuff to do', but Cimetière du Père-Lachaise is actually pretty cool. It's one of the biggest and most interesting cemeteries in Paris. After the skeletons were removed from the Cimetière des Innocents (Cemetery of Innocents) and placed in the Catacombs of Paris (SEE PaGE 46), cemeteries were banned inside the city. Several new ones were established by Napoléon I away from the city's centre at the time, and one of these was the Cimetière du Père-Lachaise. At first, nobody wanted to be buried there. People thought

it was too far from the city. So a marketing plan was developed. Basically, it involved digging up the bodies of famous people and moving them to the cemetery, so that other people would want to be buried there, too! They moved Jean de La Fontaine, France's most famous fabulist (a person who writes fables) and Molière (a famous playwright and actor). Then they moved the remains of Pierre Abélard and Héloïse, a well-known early romantic couple of the 12th century. Seems like the plan worked, too, because today this cemetery is the final resting place for many famous French writers, singers, actors and other artists, as well as some famous people from other countries.

cool, yEah?

The cemetery is named after Père François de La Chaise, who was King Louis XIV's confessor.

Jim Morrison, from the band The Doors, is buried in the Père-La-chaise Cemetery.

JUNIOR
CREEPY
ALERT
JETSET

113

tRy Not to loSE youR hEad!

Sure, Place de la Concorde might look like a beautiful, peaceful place to take a walk, but don't be fooled! It has a bloody past! This was once a public square where people were beheaded by guillotine! King Louis XVI was one of the people to be executed in the place where Place de la Concorde is today (at the time, it was called Revolution Square), but Marie-Antoinette is probably most famous for losing her head here. After the revolution, the square became a peaceful place and was renamed Place de la Concorde to symbolize the hope of a better future

cool, yEaH?

Notice anything different about this square? It's open all around!

Transporting the obelisk to Paris was really difficult. The pedestal that it stands on has some drawings explaining how it was all done.

(*concorde* means 'harmony'). An obelisk now stands in the centre of the square, precisely where the guillotine once stood. The Obelisk of Luxor was a gift from the Viceroy of Egypt. It is covered in hieroglyphics from the reign of Ramses II. The 3,300-year-old Obelisk stands 23 metres (75 feet) high, and is flanked by two large fountains. Despite the gruesome things that happened here long ago, Place de la Concorde really is one of the most beautiful and majestic places in Paris today, so don't forget your camera, especially if you are going to be there around the time of the pink-gold-red sunsets over the Seine!

115

tHE OldEst. squaREst squaRE

You'll love hanging out here! Place des Vosges is an area packed full of restaurants, cafés, art galleries, shops, hotels and plenty of cool stores with artsy stuff. The courtyard in the middle is a park with paths, fountains and grass that you can actually walk and picnic on! You probably noticed how rare that is in Paris, so take advantage of it! About 400 years ago, a square was built where Place des Vosges now stands. It was called Place Royale, but despite the square's

name, no king or queen ever lived there. The square was renamed Place des Vosges in Napoléon Bonaparte's time. Vosges, a region in the north-east of France, was the first region to pay its war taxes so, to honour the region for its good behaviour, the most beautiful square in Paris was named after it. Besides being an interesting place to visit, the square is important in history because it was the first attempt at city planning (deciding in advance which shops and buildings should be put together).

cool, yEah?

The square is really a perfect square: 140 x 140 metres.

Victor Hugo, who wrote Les Misérables and The Hunchback of Notre Dame lived in the square at number 6. His old home is now a museum.

tHE placE to SEE aNd bE SEEN

Place Vendôme might be a bit on the snobby side, but it's also a seriously stylish place to be seen! Luxury hotels, jewelers, art dealers and high-fashion shops line this famous square, and during Paris Fashion Week (SEE paGE 146), it's a hotspot for fashionistas.

King Louis XIV was responsible for ordering the construction of many grand and important buildings and monuments in and around Paris, and Place Vendôme is one of them. It was designed with buildings that were identical private residences for the rich and famous—only 27 of them! In the middle was a statue of Louis XIV on horseback. The statue stayed there until the French Revolution when a very rough 'Statue of Liberty' was put up. After one of his victories, Napoléon I ordered a statue of himself, dressed as Roman Emperor, on top of a tall column. As the political situation in France changed, so did the statue at the top of the column. Today, it's most similar to the one Napoléon put up.

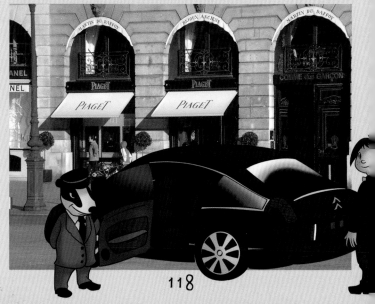

cool, yEah?

Chopin, a famous composer, lived and died at number 12 Vendôme.

Napoléon had the square's centre column made from the melted bronze of 1,200 canons captured at the Battle of Austerlitz in 1805 (just out of spite).

119

tHE HiGH poiNt of paRiS

For a spectacular view, make your way up to the dome on the roof of Basilique du Sacré-Cœur. (But be careful not to get too close to the railings! It's a long way down!) This impressive landmark stands above everything else on the highest point in the city. If you can drag yourself (and your parents) out of bed early enough, the view of the sun rising over Paris in the summer is truly unforgettable. Montmartre (the area around the hill) is traditionally known as the site of the beheading of Saint Denis. An abbey stood here for hundreds of years before it was destroyed during the French Revolution. It was only following the Franco-Prussian War of 1870–1871 that the church was built and dedicated to the Sacred Heart of Jesus.

cool, yEaH?

The church's stone bleaches itself every time it rains, which is why the basilica always looks so clean!

Artists such as Salvador Dalí, Modigliani, Claude Monet, Pablo Picasso and Vincent van Gogh all worked in the area.

Construction wasn't easy though! Costs had to be covered fully by private donations. And the ground wasn't very stable, so extremely deep foundations were needed to support the basilica, as you can still see in the catacombs. This isn't just a place for worship, though. Artists, writers, singers and various performers began flocking to Montmartre ages ago, and it soon became one of the artistic centres of the city. You can see many artists working away in one of the 76 stalls at Place du Tertre. You can also buy original artwork, but don't forget to bargain, because everything is overpriced (for tourists like you!). You'll definitely get a unique vibe when you come to this village within the city. There's even a windmill and the only vineyard in Paris!

aN iNdooR cEMEtERy foR KiNGs

How's this for creepy? According to the *Golden Legend*, after he was beheaded, Saint Denis (the first Bishop of Paris, and later the Patron Saint of France) picked up his own head and walked two miles!! In the spot where he finally stopped walking and lay down to die, the people of Paris built a church in his honour. A few centuries later, the current basilica was built on this same spot. Parts of that original church can still be seen in the crypt.

The basilica has been the burial site for almost all the French kings and many queens. This is why it's often called the 'King's Cemetery'. Unfortunately, during the French Revolution people were so mad at the monarchy that tombs were opened and the bodies were thrown into a pit outside. The tombs were saved by moving them to the Museum of French Monuments, but were eventually returned to the basilica. The bones were also returned later, but to a communal burial place in the crypt. Several kings and queens who were first buried elsewhere were moved to Saint-Denis at that time or shortly after. They include King Louis XVI and Marie-Antoinette, who were both beheaded during the revolution, as well as their son the Dauphin, King Louis XVII.

cool, yEah?

The Basilica of Saint-Denis is considered to be the first example of Gothic architecture.

Forty-three kings, 32 queens and 10 great servants of the kingdom of France are buried there.

123

taKE a stiNKy sEWER touR!

When you've had enough of fancy museums and great restaurants, go down into a Paris sewer for something totally, um… different. (And, no, we're not making this up!) The first sewers in Paris were built in the 1200s. They weren't anything like the sewers we have today, though. Instead, they were open troughs that ran down the centre of each road. Can you imagine how gross that must have been? Obviously, it wasn't the best system. Aside from being icky, it led to the spread of infections and disease. People eventually realized that an underground system was needed. The first one was built in

1370 and the system slowly expanded over the next 400 years. But these sewers weren't kept up, and sewage continued to be a problem. Napoléon I, and then Napoléon III, ordered that the sewers be improved. In 1850, separate sets of piping were installed: one set for drinking water and one set for sewage. But they also served another purpose… tourism! In fact, sewer tours were so popular that mechanical carts were installed to move all the tourists through the tunnels. Hold your nose and head on down! It's dark, damp, ugly and stinky, but you know you want to go. After all, there's even a museum and gift shop, how bad can it be!?

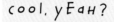

cool, yEaH?

Paris's sewers were such a well-known attraction that Victor Hugo, a famous French writer, included them in his novel, Les Misérables.

Mechanical carts in the sewers were replaced by full trolleys, making them one of the earliest 'subway' systems.

cool, yEah?

The year the stadium was built (1998) France went on to win the World Cup for the first time ever. They beat the invincible Brazil team 3-0!!

Constructing this mammoth took only 31 months!

hEy, all you football faNs!

Like most European cities, Paris takes its football (soccer) seriously. When France was picked to host the 1998 World Cup, a new stadium was needed, but there were two specific requirements. It had to give 80,000 fans a dry place to sit in case of rain and it had to have real grass on the pitch. The solution they came up with is one really cool roof. Part of it is made of a special glass that filters out red and infrared light rays but lets in the blue and green rays needed to grow grass.

The field can also be rearranged to have a running track, which was necessary when the 2003 World Championships in Athletics were held in the stadium. It's also a popular place for mega rock concerts. Ideally, try to catch a game (any game) in the stadium and enjoy the party atmosphere, the drumming, the singing and the colourful fans. And if you can't do that, at least check out the museum and take a tour to learn about the stadium's history and construction. You'll love every second of it, but you'll be especially impressed by the sheer hugeness of the place!

tHE moSt bEautiful viEw FRom tHE uGly-duckLiNG toweR

The view from the Eiffel Tower is spectacular, but there's just one little problem: you can't see the tower if you're in it! What to do, what to do? You could try the Sacré-Cœur hill (SEE paGE 120) or a balloon ride at the Parc André Citroën (SEE paGE 158). Or you could just head on over to the second-tallest structure in Paris—the Tour Montparnasse! Paris has lots of strict and specific rules about how buildings look and where they can be built. That's a way of keeping the streets and the city looking as beautiful as it does. Napoléon III hired Baron Haussmann, a French civic planner, to modernize the city, building large roadways and magnificent monuments all over Paris. Many of the important, historic landmarks you see in Paris today are the result of his efforts.

cool, yEaH?

Alain 'Spiderman' Robert once scaled the tower using only his bare hands and feet, with no safety devices. He has also climbed other tall buildings all over the world. He is usually arrested as soon as he gets to the roof!

The helipad on the rooftop platform is for emergencies only (for instance, if the President comes visit).

After World War II, there was another phase of modernization in Paris. This time, the focus was on building major office towers. The first one was the Tour Montparnasse, but once it was built, it instantly became unpopular. People thought it was unattractive and that

it stood out in the skyline too much. So, shortly after, all other skyscrapers were banished to the outskirts of Paris, mainly to La Défense (SEE paGE 108). Parisians even have a joke about Montparnasse: the best view in Paris is from the tower, because that way, you don't have to look at it! But whatever you think of the building itself, there's no arguing with the fact that the views really are breathtaking. Besides, it has the coolest express elevator, showing your progress on a TV screen, as you dart up to the 56th floor.

'Tuileries' is the French word for tilery—a factory or kiln for making tiles.

There's talk of rebuilding the Palais des Tuileries. It could be used to expand the Louvre Museum!

a GaRdEN fit foR Royalty

The Jardin des Tuileries is a beautiful place to take a walk. In fact, it's fit for royalty, which isn't surprising once you learn that it's on land where a palace once stood! Five hundred years ago, during the Middle Ages, a clay quarry took up the space where the Jardin des Tuileries is today. With the quarry were several tile factories. When King Henry II died, his widow, Catherine de Médicis—who was Italian—decided to build a new palace along with an Italian-style garden. A hundred years later, the garden was redesigned and became a typical French garden, with paths, terraces, pools, fountains, hedges and sculptures. Important note: like in most classical parks in Paris, you're not allowed to walk on the grass!

When the royal family moved out of Paris, the palace and gardens were used as a theatre and a fashionable promenade for wealthy Parisians. At one time, there were even cafés, kiosks, merry-go-rounds, deck chairs and public toilets! In 1871, the palace was destroyed by a fire and the garden was expanded. Two buildings that were constructed in 1861 survived and are now museums: the Galerie Nationale du Jeu de Paume and the Musée de l'Orangerie.

131

a zoo with no baRs on caGEs!!!

Universal Expositions weren't the only expositions held
in Paris. The 1931 Paris Colonial Exposition highlighted
different cultures from all over the world. The event was held
in the Bois de Vincennes, just outside Paris, and one of its
features was a small temporary zoo with exotic animals. The
temporary zoo was so popular, though, that a permanent
zoo was created in the same place. Zoo de Vincennes was
designed to make people feel like they were standing right
next to the animals. We're serious!! There are no bars here,
because animals either are not dangerous or, if they are,

cool, yEaH?

**Be sure to climb the 65-metre
'Grand Rocher'. At the top of this
rocky hill, you'll get a great view of
the city, and the zoo.**

**About 1,400 animals live there!
This includes arctic wolves,
giraffes and hippopotami.**

there is a buffer space between you and them (like a moat). Most of the animals belong to nearly extinct species whose natural environments have been destroyed. They're not just on display; they also play an important role in biodiversity and conservation. The zoo has about 150 animal births every year, which is a real feat for some species where every single animal counts! Once animals become extinct in the wild, they can only be re-introduced if there are babies born in zoos. You can't miss Nocturama, where you can get a really good look at the nocturnal lemurs living normally without human interference.

133

you'll have a whale of a time!

If you're craving beach and water fun during your vacation, head over to Aquaboulevard, an indoor and outdoor water park. You can enjoy the tropics all year round in the largest water park in Europe with swimming pools, water rides, tunnels and slides. Surrounding these attractions are fountains, waterfalls, a river and exotic trees. You also can't miss the life-sized model of a whale.

If you want to learn to body surf, try the wave pool—the waves aren't huge but should be enough to get the basics. And if you like waterslides you've come to the right place. The Aquaturbo provides some serious speed. Or, for something a bit more relaxing, the longer Aquaplouf might be just right. If the weather is good, grab your sunscreen and head outside where there's a pool, a large artificial beach and even grassy areas to play on (and, yes, you're actually allowed to step on this grass!).

The complex also offers tennis and squash courts and a fitness centre and gym. End your visit by catching a film at the cinema and grabbing a meal at one of the restaurants. You'll probably need this downtime to relax after such exhausting fun!

cool, yEah?

The temperature is permanently set at a very balmy 29ºC (84ºF).

The 27-metre (90-foot) whale was an art piece commissioned by Captain Jacques Cousteau, the famous French ocean explorer.

MoRE thaN just a FEw ways to GEt FRom HERE to tHERE

You'll definitely need to get around town during your visit and, lucky for you, there are lots of ways! Of course, the best way to get familiar with any area is the old-fashioned way— walking! Walking lets you discover every nook and cranny, including small shops and cafés that you might otherwise miss. Or, if you need to get somewhere fast, the Paris Métro is a great choice. There are 300 stations, 16 different lines, 214 km of tracks and 384 stops; making it possible to get from wherever you are to anywhere you want to go. Just avoid rush hour, if you can, unless you like to be squeezed like a canned sardine. You could even spend your day just touring the Métro system, which has some really cool stations–but watch out, it could be addictive!

The River Seine is an important part of Paris, so why not use it to get from one place to another? There are tours available (SEE batEauX MoucHES - PagE 138), or for something a bit more practical, try the Batobus, a convenient hop-on-hop-off way to get to some of the most important sights of Paris. The basic ticket is a 1-day pass. You'll also notice bicycle stations all over the city. They're called Velib' and they're part of the city's public bicycle rental program. You can take a bike from one station for the day, go where you need, and then leave the bike at another station. There are 20,000 bikes all over Paris, although it may be hard to find a bike or a parking spot in rush hour, at least in some areas. You do have to be at least 14 years old to use the bikes, though...

cool, yEaH?

For something really special and out of the ordinary, there are horse and carriage rides around the city, especially near parks and palaces.

SEE tHE SiGHts fROm a fRESH pERspEctivE: batEau, aHoy!

It makes sense that the River Seine, which cuts through the centre of Paris, is a major waterway for the city. Many of the first people to live in Paris arrived by boat thousands of years ago. A lot has changed since then, but the city centre has always remained by the river side, in the Île-de-la-Cité. Some of the oldest historic buildings and monuments stand there.

The first company to offer riverboat cruises was Compagnie des Bateaux Mouches. This term became so popular that people eventually started calling any boat tours 'bateaux mouches'. Nowadays, there are plenty of other riverboat cruise companies in Paris (Vedettes de Paris, Vedettes du Pont Neuf, Batobus, and more—you can find a complete list of river tour companies in the reference section at the end of this book). On a boat tour, you'll see the riverside sights from a completely new perspective: the Eiffel Tower, Les Invalides, the Louvre and Notre Dame, to name a few. You'll also see all the cool bridges that cross the Seine. There are 37 of them in the city! Some boat companies even offer hop-on-hop-off services that work like river buses, so you can tour some sights you haven't seen along the way. And the last tip: take your tour at night if you want to see the city lights, especially the Eiffel Tower's cool light shows. That's a must!

cool, yEaH?

'Bateaux mouches' translates as 'fly boats', but they aren't named after an insect, rather after the area where the first boats were made. (The first was a steam boat left from the Universal Exhibition.)

cool, yEah?

> *Café Procope is still around today. You'll find it at 13, rue de l'Ancienne-Comedie.*

There's a French word for people who choose a terrace and then stay there for hours, only ordering a coffee or a shake: they're called Monsieur Terrace or flaneurs!

GEt comfy at a local bistRo

If there's a coffee shop on practically every corner in the city where you live, you've got Paris to thank. The world's first café opened here in 1674. It was called Café Procope and was so successful that, in 1686, it moved to a bigger space. Cafés have thrived in the city ever since!

Even if you hate the smell of your parents' coffee, you can't go to Paris and not sit in a café terrace, a bistro, a pâtisserie or a restaurant. Everyone does it: the young, the old, the rich, the poor, the famous, the infamous, politicians, actors, teachers and students. Writers are especially famous for spending hours hanging out in cafés. Ernest Hemingway wrote *The Sun also Rises* in a Paris café. James Joyce also wrote in one. And Victor Hugo spent so much time socializing in cafés that he barely had time to write! Grab a chair at the nearest one (outside if the weather is good), order a juice or a fancy milkshake and sit back to people-watch. Who knows, maybe you'll even see an intriguing character walk by and be inspired to pick up a pen and write a book of your own!

CaN CaN CaN you do tHE CaNCaN?

The Moulin Rouge was opened in 1889, near Montmartre. This cabaret, which looks just like a big red windmill, is the birthplace of today's cancan. The cancan is a type of dance that is performed by several dancers in a chorus-line. This physically demanding and tiring dance involves high kicks, circular leg movements, knee lifts, standing on one leg, cartwheels and flying splits—all while wearing feathers, sequins, stockings, petticoats and long skirts with heavy frills. Talk about complicated!

The cancan isn't the only type of cabaret or variety show you might see in Paris, though. Common acts include comedians, mimes, singers, dancers, jugglers, acrobats, clowns and people who do strange stuff. Actually, sometimes you can see a variety of these all in one show—which is why these shows are called *varieté*! One thing all of them have in common, though, is that they're usually performed on a high stage, with a funny master of ceremonies presenting the acts to an audience sitting at tables, eating and drinking. Some places are really fancy, while others are more relaxed, but this type of show is classic Paris entertainment. You'll laugh, clap, stomp your feet and leave in a really good mood! And here's an extra: if you ask for a table at the front you can almost be sure some crazy comedian will single you out and bring you into the act (which could be good fun).

cool, yEah?

Many of Henri de Toulouse-Lautrec's (a French painter and print maker) works were inspired by the cancan and the Moulin Rouge.

The cancan was once considered quite scandalous and risqué.

GEt CauGHt uP iN a CiRCuS act

Animals, acrobats, jugglers, tightrope walkers, flying trapeze
artists and more… When it comes to the circus, Paris
doesn't clown around. In fact, the city has two permanent
circuses: Cirque d'Hiver and Cirque Diana Moreno Bormann.
When you think of the circus, you probably think of huge
tents—but it wasn't always this way. At one time, large
structures were built specifically for the circus. They were
usually round or oval to accommodate the ring for the
performers. The Cirque d'Hiver (Winter Circus), started by
Napoléon III in 1852, is one circus like this. The shows in the

building change constantly, so there's always something new to see. Aside from regular circus acts, the Cirque d'Hiver also has horse shows, concerts, fashion shows and other events. If you're a real circus freak, you'll also want to see the Cirque Diana Moreno Bormann, a family-run circus and the largest animal circus in Paris. All the tigers, elephants, zebras, dogs, camels, ostriches, ponies, yaks, snakes and doves are treated like family there. You can even visit the animals to learn how they're taken care of and trained. You'll also see how the circus equipment is installed, how performers put on their make-up and how the props are used.

cool, yEaH?

Cirque d'Hiver was originally called Cirque Napoléon (the name only changed in 1870).

The Cirque d'Hiver building isn't actually an oval, but has 20 sides that make it appear oval-shaped. Can you spot it?

SEE SOME CYCLING OR GO FOR GLITZ AND GLAMOUR

The name Tour de France means 'around France' and this famous bike race sees the world's top cyclists biking all around the country. Every year, the course changes, but it always ends in Paris on the Champs-Élysées. The tour started out as a marketing campaign for *L'Auto* sports newspaper. Back then, single bicyclists participated and anyone could enter. Today, the race has about 20–22 teams of nine riders, and it is by invitation only. Teams really have to be the best of the best if they want to make it in and have a shot at winning those trophies and the yellow shirts given as prizes. It's the biggest summer event in the country.

With designers like Chanel, Christian Dior, Jean-Paul Gaultier, Hermès, Christian Lacroix, Yves Saint-Laurent and Louis Vuitton, is it any surprise that Paris is one of the world's fashion capitals? Twice a year, top designers from France and all over the world come to Paris to display their fashions for the next season. Some designers create really strange, edgy, almost wacky clothes—the kind you doubt anyone would actually wear! But when you add the catwalks, the bright lights and the flashy jewelry it adds up to instant glamour...

cool, yeah?

The Tour de France takes three weeks and covers over 3,500 km (2,200 miles)

The most important fashion weeks are held in Paris, Milan, London and New York City, but nowadays most large cities have them.

ONE Kid's tRasH is aNotHER Kid's tREasuRE...

The things you'll find at the Paris flea markets are a long way from being trash or junk, but when the first flea markets started, more than 200 years ago, they actually did sell stuff that people found in the garbage! Today's flea markets are much more organized and sell almost everything, even though they often have specialties. For example, some sell antiques, old toys and old books. Others sell vintage clothing and jewelry.

There are four main flea markets in Paris today: Les Puces de St-Ouen (the largest, just outside the city) which actually has 13 specialized markets; Puces de la Porte de Vanves (an outdoor market); Marché Beauvau (the least expensive); and Puces de Montreuil (which also offers car parts and machines). For something a little different, there's Orphelins-Apprentis d'Auteuil. Proceeds from sales at this little-known boutique support the orphan charity that organizes it. Whichever one you choose, you'll definitely want to check out at least one of Paris's flea markets before heading home. You're guaranteed to find something unique, and probably no fleas at all (but we're not making promises)!

Tip: Hide your wallet and anything you value… just in case. Your passport should stay safely stored, or your parents should carry it.

cool, yEaH?

The best time to go is in the morning. Flea markets get crowded in the afternoon.

It's all about haggling, so drive your hardest bargain. You're sure to get a great discount!

food tastes way better when you call it 'cuisine!'

Wherever you travel, everyone loves a good meal, but the French are especially well-known for their food. It was France, and more specifically Paris, that invented the modern restaurant for the world! So it should come as no surprise, then, that Paris is home to many well-known chefs and restaurants, and even to the most popular restaurant travel book series, the Michelin Guides. The Michelin awards talented chefs and outstanding restaurants with one, two or

three stars. These are the best restaurants (and chefs!) anywhere in the world! So why not learn where the experts once learned, and spend a few hours at l'École Lenôtre? Whether you're already a whiz in the kitchen, or just getting started, it's a great place to learn the basics of French cuisine. You'll leave prepared to impress your mom and dad with a perfect *tarte niçoise* or *confit de verdures*. Plus, at the end of the class, you get to eat what you've created! Did dinner ever taste so good? **PS:** You need to speak and understand at least a bit of French.

cool, yEah?

France has more Michelin starred restaurants and chefs than any other country. (And they're really very proud of it!)

Great chefs are known to work in busy, messy kitchens but never-ever spill any food on their pristine white coats... now, that's impressive!

lEavE youR paRENts at tHE dooR. tHEN GEt REAdy FoR fuN!

For 800 years, Les Halles was the spot of Paris's central open-air food market. In its place, today, you'll find the Forum des Halles (a large underground shopping centre) and the Jardin des Halles (the garden above it). The garden has a waterfall, grassy areas, play areas, a merry-go-round, a vegetable garden, a tropical greenhouse and… the best part… the Jardin des Enfants. The Jardin des Enfants is a kids' park, and it's **only** for kids! That's right, no parents or adults allowed, except for the staff in charge of the site and

kids! Tell your mom and dad to go grab a café au lait, then leave them at the door for one session of sheer fun (each ticket allows you to stay about one hour)! There are six 'worlds' including: *le monde sonore* (world of sounds), *le monde mou* (soft world), *le monde tropical* (tropical world) and *l'île mystérieuse* (mystery island). Get lost in the bamboo forest, or climb the ropes or climbing walls. Or take a trip down the slides, through the tunnels or through the maze. This is a popular place, so to avoid a disappointing surprise it might be a good idea to have your parents reserve your tickets ahead of time, or you'll miss out on the fun!

cool, yEah?

The sculpture 'Ecoute' (Listen) that you'll see in the park is of a giant head resting on a hand. It's made of sandstone and weighs 70 tons!!

There are lots of lawns in Les Halles where you can have a picnic or soak up some sun.

153

cool, yEah?

*Even though the name makes it sound that way,
opéra comique isn't always comic.*

*Bees on the roof of the Palais Garnier produce honey
that is sold to (expensive) Paris food shops.*

*The French Revolution started at the Bastille fortress-
prison–people gathered around, freed the prisoners (all 7
of them!) and then burnt it down to the ground.*

aRia REAdy FoR SomE opERa?

What would you rather do: spend an hour listening to somebody scratch their fingernails down a chalkboard, or spend an hour at the opera? Tough call? Okay, now admit it, have you ever actually been to an opera? Seriously, don't knock it until you've tried it! You might just surprise yourself by loving it!

The art form of opera became popular in Paris in the time of King Louis XIV. During the revolution, traditional opera almost disappeared while *opéra comique* (a type which includes spoken dialogue) survived. Later, Napoléon I decreased the number of opera houses to three: the Opéra, Opéra-Comique and Théâtre-Italien.

Today, several opera houses exist in Paris. The largest are the Palais Garnier and Opéra de la Bastille. The Palais Garnier, an architectural landmark, was completed in 1875. It took longer than expected to build because the area sat above an underground lake. Have you ever seen *The Phantom of the Opera*? If so, this might sound familiar to you. This opera house above a lake was the inspiration for the musical. The Opéra de la Bastille, on the other hand, is a larger, more modern opera house and is the favourite theatre for opera these days. It also stands in a historic square, where the Bastille fortress-prison once stood! It is nowadays one of the most popular meeting places in the city!

155

GEt yOuR GamE oN!

Chaud Devant? *Cocotaki*? *Kleine Fische*? These might sound like exotic food items, but if you come to Oya café expecting to order from the menu, be prepared to be surprised. Oya doesn't serve meals (although you can get drinks and snacks). The specialty here is games! Lots and lots of board games! Board games from floor to ceiling! Games from all over the world! You can watch them, play them or even buy them. For a small fee, pick your own

cool, yEah?

Don't worry about not being able to read instructions in a foreign language! The staff at Oya are familiar with ALL of their games, and they'll explain everything.

There are over 250 games!

game to try or, if you're having a hard time deciding, just ask the staff for advice. Tell them what you like and they'll help you find just the right thing. Or, why not take our suggestion? You're in Paris, after all, so why not give *Métro*— a game based on Paris's Métro system—a try? The Oya café is also a really good place to meet people. Wednesdays are an especially great night to visit with your parents if you're looking to play with some of the locals, and maybe make some acquaintances that will give you more Paris tips!

GEt a biRd's-EyE viEw of paRis...iN a HElium ballooN!

Paris isn't a city known for its green spaces, but the André Citroën Park is one exception. Here, you can actually relax on the grass! Check out the Jardin Blanc (White Garden), which has all white flowers; the Jardin Noir (Black Garden), which has all dark flowers; the six Jardins Seriels (Serial Gardens), which have distinctive designs; and the Jardin en Mouvement (Garden in Movement), where different grasses move in the wind. You can also see greenhouses, a reflecting pool, a play area and fountains. But the coolest thing in the park has got to be the Ballon Air de Paris—a helium-filled balloon that rises 150 metres (490 feet) in the air, giving you one of the best views of the city.

The land where the park stands also has an interesting history. For a few hundred years, the village of Javel stood surrounded by grassy fields. But, in 1785, a chemist called Claude Louis Berthollet discovered the powerful bleaching properties of chlorine, and soon a bleach factory was built on part of the fields. The remaining fields became the huge manufacturing plant for the French car-maker, Citroën. In 1990, both factories were torn down to create this great park.

cool, yEaH?

Nowadays, bleach is still called 'eau de Javel' (water of Javel) in French.

The Ballon Air de Paris changes colour according to the quality of the air—green for good, orange for medium and red for poor. On a clear day, from the balloon's gondola, you can see 30 kilometres out.

taKE tHE HiGH Road iN paRis

The Promenade Plantée—an elevated park and walkway—is a truly awesome place to take a walk. Built on what was once an old railroad track and viaduct (a type of bridge), it stretches from Place de la Bastille almost all the way to one of Paris's largest parks, the Bois de Vincennes (SEE PaGE 40). Underneath the viaduct, you'll find arts and crafts workshops, galleries, furniture showrooms and cafés.

cool, yEaH?

The promenade is also called the Coulée Vert ('the Green Flow').

Only about 1.5 km of the 4.5 km promenade is elevated.

Above the shops is the promenade, with a path lined with plants. It's a great place for a jog, or to skate or bike. And the view of the streets below is definitely something not to be missed. The elevated section of the promenade also travels along, beside and almost through buildings (it feels like it, anyway!), and ends at the Jardin de Reuilly, a garden with terraces, a playground, statues, roses and a café. For sure this is one of the most unique parks we've come across!

cool, yEaH?

'Guignol' is often used as an insult, meaning 'buffoon'.
It doesn't make much sense, though, since Guignol is
actually clever, witty, courageous and generous!

The character Guignol was so popular that, these days,
the term 'guignol' describes any puppet show!

MEEt GuiGNOl: paRis's MoSt faMOUS pUppEt

Do you love going to the dentist? Would you want to go more often if your dentist provided free entertainment? This is what dentist Laurent Mourguet was hoping for when he started the marionette and puppet tradition in Paris as a way to attract patients into his office. His first puppet show was based on an Italian comedy, Pulcinella. Pulcinella was a character with a long nose that looked like a bird's beak. He dressed in white and wore a black mask. This same character appeared all over Europe, although each country changed his name, looks and clothing a little. In England he was called Punchinello (or Punch, of Punch and Judy). Eventually, Mourguet gave up dentistry to become a full-time puppeteer. He wanted to create his own characters that his French audience would be able to relate to more easily, so Guignol was born. This famous puppet has been entertaining audiences ever since. There are several places to see a puppet show in Paris: Jardin des Tuileries (SEE PaGE 130), Jardin du Luxembourg (SEE PaGE 74), Jardin d'Acclimatation (SEE PaGE 68), and Champ de Mars all have puppet theatres. Or, if you're lucky enough, someone will put up a makeshift puppet show in the Métro, in-between two stops. Those are usually as awesome as they are unexpected and surprising, so get your act together and donate a big euro coin at the end of the show and shout out a 'bravo'!

163

bE paRt of a GiaNt RollERbladE paRadE, but REMEMbER to kit-up

If you want to see Paris the way the locals do, skip the stuffy tour bus and strap on your rollerblades. Rollers et Coquillages is a group that gathers for short and long skating events all over the city. You don't need to be an expert rollerblader to join in the fun, but you do need to have some experience. (As long as you can stay on your feet most of the time, you'll be fine!) It's a relaxing and fun thing to do on a Sunday afternoon.

The Rollers et Coquillages staff always leads the pack of 10,000 or so skaters, following a police motorcade through the empty streets of Paris. In case you're wondering why the streets are empty and why the police are tagging along, it's because the organizers have to submit a route to the central *gendarmerie* (police station), so the police can close off the necessary roads to accommodate all the skaters. They even send an escort of officers on roller-skates and bikes, wearing cool sporty uniforms. The route, which starts and ends in Place de la Bastille, changes every time, so it really is a one-of-a-kind experience.

cool, yEaH?

Did you know that skaters are nicknamed 'shellfish'?

No worries about losing your way. With thousands of you, just follow the crowd. Or, stick to the staff, which are the ones in the bright yellow T-shirts.

165

ENjoy a stRoll by thE RivERsidE

The River Seine has always been an important part of Paris, and many of the city's most famous landmarks were built on its banks, like Notre Dame, the Louvre and the Eiffel Tower. The river divides the city into two sides. The Rive Gauche (lEft baNk) is the southern bank. It's full of young artists, writers and intellectuals. They've helped the area get the reputation of being a hip, cool place. The Rive Droite (RiGht baNk) is the northern bank and it's considered the more sophisticated and commercial side. In the middle of the river you'll find Île-de-la-Cité and Île Saint-Louis, with their very unique characters (SEE paGE 66). In 1991, the banks of the Seine were added to the United Nations' list of World Heritage Sites in Europe. This was even before Paris Plage (a fake beach on the Seine, every summer)! You always hear that Paris is best seen on foot, and there's really no better way than walking all the way across the city, following the river. You'll never forget about that time you crossed

the whole of Paris by foot, and you even get bragging rights! If you get tired and need a lift, riverboat cruises leave from spots all along the riverbanks (SEE all about boats oN pagES 136 to 139). Besides, you can always stop for a snack at some of the café-boats docked along the quays, and read one of the old books you bought!

cool, yEaH?

Over the centuries, the River Seine has inspired many artists, such as painters Claude Monet and Georges Seurat. Victor Hugo even used the Seine's riverbanks as the setting for his character's escape in the novel Les Misérables.

Napoléon Bonaparte wanted to be buried on the banks of the River Seine. Needless to say, after being banished to Saint Helena, he was lucky enough they allowed him to be buried in France!

take to the treetops like an ape

If you like climbing in trees and acting like a monkey, don't miss this one! At Atout Branches, you'll take to the treetops of a mighty forest, then move through the air from tree to tree along bridges, ropes, nets and tubes. Sometimes, you'll find yourself as high as 12 metres (39 feet) off the ground.

If you've never tried it before, don't worry. Your adventure will start with a course in climbing techniques where you'll learn how to play here safely. Helmets and harnesses are a must. The courses vary in difficulty, so there's something for everyone, from super-easy to truly-tough.

cool, yEah?

One of the courses is equipped with automatic safety devices —perfect for younger kids!

JUNIOR
REALLY
COOL!
JETSETTERS

city of lights and perfume

Just a short drive from Paris, you'll find the town of Chartres. It's best known as the capital of light and perfume, thanks to the Festival of Lights and the number of perfume shops in the area.

The town dates back over a thousand years! The most important building there is the Cathédrale Notre-Dame de Chartres (Cathedral of Our Lady of Chartres). The cathedral was destroyed and rebuilt several times over the last millennium and has been the focal point of almost every town activity, including a market, a school and a meeting place. Today, despite its small size, Chartres has tons to offer visitors. In local markets you'll find food and clothing, and there's a cool Christmas Market each year.

If it's museums you want to see, check out the Fine Arts Museum, Agriculture Museum, School Museum, Stained Glass Centre or Archæology Museum. And definitely don't miss Picassiette House. It's a house completely decorated with mosaics of broken china and pottery. Artist studios in Chartres specialize in stained glass, sculpture, mosaics, calligraphy and illumination and painting, and often offer workshops for kids. Make sure you also try some of the city's food specialties, like *Chartres Pâté*, *Poule au Pot* or *Sablé du Beauce*.

cool, yeah?

Vikings once controlled the town of Chartres.

King Henry IV was crowned King of France in Chartres, making him one of the few French kings not to be crowned in the Cathedral of Reims.

171

it's just a 'simple' Royal lodge...

Château de Fontainebleau is one of the biggest royal castles in Paris. It was first built by King François I and was mostly used as a place for kings to stay during the hunting season—kind of like a giant (and very fancy) lodge! But, over the centuries, many different kings and queens lived in the castle, and each one added to it in their own way. Catherine de Médicis, King Henry IV and Napoléon I were some of the famous rulers who lived in, and renovated, the castle.

Because of this, the castle is a mix of different styles, and walking through can feel a bit like a French history lesson! There are some fun activities to do at the château. Horse drawn carriage rides and *jeu de paume* ('real tennis') demonstrations are just two of them. The surrounding forest (once the hunting grounds used by royalty) is now a national park with a conservation mission and is home to many birds, mammals and butterflies. It's also a great place for hikers, walkers, horseback riders, rock-climbers and mountain bikers.

cool, yEah?

Leonardo da Vinci spent some time at the Château de Fontainebleau.

Da Vinci's Mona Lisa was exhibited for the very first time at Fontainebleau when King François I bought it.

173

tHE palacE of tHE SuN KiNG

Paris wasn't always a democracy (a government elected by the people). King Louis XIV, the Sun King, believed that all the power was his (this was called absolute monarchy). In an effort to gain more control, he moved his court and government to Versailles, away from the people of Paris. The Sun King believed that France revolved around him, so his palace had to be impressive.

Louis XIV was a stickler for rules and etiquette. He even had rules and procedures for when he got up in the morning. This was called *Lever*, or ceremonial rising, and began at 8:30am. Only a few important people were allowed to see the king in the morning (doctors, family and maybe some friends) while he was washed, combed and shaven by his bedroom staff. This was *le Petit Lever*. *Le Grand Lever* followed, when the king was dressed and ate breakfast. Important officials were invited for this. The rest of the day followed a tight schedule as well, including *Coucher*, which was basically the Lever in reverse before bed.

While he lived at Château de Versailles, Louis XIV expanded the palace a lot. His plans were so huge that new marble quarries were needed to supply materials for the palace's construction. New factories were also opened to produce silk, porcelain and mirrors for the interior. The royal family was forced to return to Paris during the French Revolution. By that time, it was Louis XVI, the Sun King's grandson who lived in the palace. During the revolution, most of the palace's contents were auctioned off and the palace was placed under the Republic's control. Today it is an unforgettable symbol of the once absolute kingdom of France.

174

cool, yEah?

One of the peace treaties that ended World War I was signed in the palace. It's called the Treaty of Versailles.

King Louis XVI gave the Petit Trianon (a small château on the estate) to his wife, Marie-Antoinette, in 1774. She used it to escape the royal responsibilities she had in Paris.

175

FROM AN ASTERIX VILLAGE TO THE MYSTERY OF MONT SAINT-MICHEL

Normandy is a province in northern France, on the coast across the channel from Great Britain. It has a unique identity and a past that's really different from that of Paris. People are very proud of their heritage and independence there, and often make a point of speaking their own language—Norman-French. Normandy is a big region. It's also really pretty, with winding roads, rolling fields, beautiful seascapes and fishing villages. The highlight is Mont Saint-Michel, a huge castle-like fortress rising out of the sea on a rocky island. You can get to it by land in low tides or by boat in high tide.

There are lots of other towns and ports worth visiting in Normandy. The port of Le Havre is an exciting place. So is the picturesque village of Etratat, a beautiful stony beach nestled between two cliffs, with great views and yummy restaurants. Up the coast are the twin towns of Deauville and Trouville—both historic beach destinations. Honfleur, an 11th century fishing port with a well-preserved centre, seems to come out of an Astérix book! The area around the Old Dock is especially nice with its historic narrow houses, museums and gardens. If you have an hour to spare, try Geocaching—a treasure-hunting game where adventurers use the Internet and GPS devices to find hidden prizes around town. You'll need your parents' help for this one!

But the coast of Normandy is more well-known for what went on during World War II. Its beautiful sandy beaches with wild waves were once the most ferocious battlefield in Europe. On 6 June 1944, American, British and Canadian troops landed there to liberate the continent from the Nazis. Operation Overlord was the greatest seaborne invasion ever. The day marked a turning point in World War II. You can go along the frontlines with your parents by following 'Overlord' or 'Pegasus' road signs on the village-hopping coastal roads.

coast of NoRmandy
Côte de Normandie

say bonjouR to micKEy mousE!

When you arrive at the Disneyland Resort, hop on the Disneyland Railroad and travel between the five separate 'lands' in the park. Main Street, USA is a 1920s small town complete with a city hall, horse-drawn streetcars and arcades. Frontierland is a trip back in time to the American West of the 1800s, with cowboys, pioneers, saloons, gold rushes, an Indian village and even riverboats! Adventureland takes you to the remote jungles of Asia, the Caribbean and the South Pacific. Fantasyland is a fairy tale village, based on Disney movies, and Discoveryland is the land of tomorrow—science fiction and the future are the themes there. The resort also includes Walt Disney Studios Park, which is based on a real-life animated film studio. Rides and roller-coasters are mixed with shows, special effects and stunts. It's all good fun for a day, a weekend or a week!

cool, yEah?

The entire park is about one-fifth the size of Paris! How wild is that!?

Disneyland Resort Paris is one of only five Disney parks in the world (the others are in Los Angeles, Florida, Tokyo and Hong Kong!

a day of old-fashioned family fun at the rides and jousting

Fami Parc is an old-fashioned family-oriented amusement park located in Seine-et-Marne, just outside Paris. There's something for kids of every age and size—whether you're seeking big thrills, or quieter rides! Try the bumpy 15-metre-high roller-coaster, the speedy pirate ship, the soaked-in-fun wild river log ride or the quaint and colourful carousels.

And, once you've had your fill of rides, slow down and catch a show. Every day of the summer the park puts on live shows for kids and adults. The shows are always changing, but to give you an idea, you might see a show focused on medieval times, or a jousting tournament where horses and knights clad in colourful gowns really ride against each other. You might also see a sword contest based on D'Artagnan's *Three Musketeers*; or an impressive falconry show, exhibiting the skills of huge birds of prey, trained to land in their master's leather-gloved hand! Besides, there's also plenty of green space to walk around, and lots of wildlife to see, like ducks, geese, swans and perhaps even a river otter.

cool, yEaH?

D'Artagnan and the three musketeers of the king were not real characters, although they are based on real musketeers of the king!

Jousting was a medieval tournament sport played by armoured knights on horses. They used a variety of weapons, such as tilting with a lance, blows with the battle-axe, strokes with the dagger or strokes with a sword.

Falconry can be performed with any type of bird of prey, usually an eagle, falcon, hawk or owl.

SEE FRANCE IN NO TIME FLAT!

France Miniature is an amusement park with a twist. Sure, there are plenty of rides, but it's also got *all* of France! The park is shaped just like France and contains 116 of the most interesting, most important and most awesome monuments and landmarks, placed in their appropriate spots. Like France itself, the park borders on the 'Atlantic Ocean' and the 'Mediterranean Sea'. And there's more! Head into the indoor exhibition where the interiors of 50 unusual and prestigious places are reproduced down to the teeniest, tiniest details. Where else can you walk from one side of France to the other in just a few minutes?

cool, yEah?

The park has the world's longest outdoor miniature railway network. It's 3.5 kilometres long and has 13 trains.

France Miniature has 20,000 miniature trees, 15 rivers, five acres of sea and more than 100 boats and ships, as well as a motorway with moving vehicles.

cool, yEah?

The château and stables appeared in the James Bond film 'A View to a Kill'.

The stables have enough room for 240 horses and about 500 dogs.

184

spot thE HoRSE-pRiNCE...?

One of King Louis XIV's grandsons, Louis-Henri de Bourbon, loved horses. He loved them so much, actually, that he believed when he died, he would be reincarnated as one! That's why he built the Grand Stables—as a place he thought would be suitable for him to live in his next life. Whether he actually got reincarnated as a horse or not, the end result is a masterpiece of 18th century architecture, considered to be the most beautiful stables in the world.

Many years later, the estate (including its châteaus, stables and gardens) was donated to the Institut de France in the hopes that it would be preserved, and the Living Horse Museum was created inside the Grand Stables. This museum features live horses that follow specific trotting routines and perform demonstrations with riders, dressed in costume. Learn how the different breeds vary and which breeds were used by the princes back in the 18th century. And keep an eye out for Louis-Henri while you're there! You never know...

calliNG all you cowboys aNd cowgiRls out tHERE!

When you think of the Wild West, you probably picture American cowboys and Indians... but you might be surprised to learn that France actually helped the US expand west. When Napoléon Bonaparte sold Louisiana to the United States, he gave Americans the opportunity to head west to set up farms and start new lives. Others headed west during the gold rush. The West wasn't a gentle place. First, there were the wars between some of the newcomers, the American cowboys and the Native Americans (at that time called 'Indians') who were protecting their land. Then there were the outlaws. Everyone has heard of Jesse James, Billy the Kid and Butch Cassidy.

Mer de Sable is a theme park based on this time in history. The desert environment, cowboys on horses and the locomotives all help to recreate the Wild West. There are rodeos, shows, trains, rides, roller-coasters and water rides, all with a western feel to them. The park is divided into three main areas: the Desert, the Jungle (forest) and the Time of Pioneers. Each area is dedicated to a different part of the Wild West, so there's plenty to enjoy!

cool, yEah?

Mer de Sable was the first theme park in France.

The Wild West is known for the struggle between the Law (which was often weak) and bandits. The most famous gunfight of the time was the Gunfight at the O.K. Corral (which didn't actually happen at the O.K. Corral!).

wHERE comic books come to lifE

Chances are, you've heard of *Astérix the Gaul*—the extremely famous (not to mention funny) series of comics about two friends, Astérix and his sidekick, Obélix. But what you might not have heard before is that the series is broadly based on real events in the Roman times.

Long before it became the place it is today, France included part of an area called Gaul. About two thousand years ago, the army of Julius Caesar's Rome invaded Gaul and conquered most of the region, inhabited by 'Barbarians', as the Romans called them. Signs of the Roman occupation can still be seen throughout Paris today. And it was this invasion that inspired two men, Goscinny and Uderzo, to create *The Adventures of Astérix* (*Astérix le Gaulois*). In the comics, the village's druid creates a magic potion that gives them superhuman strength, helping Astérix, the smallest of the Gauls, to fend off the Romans. The series follows the two friends on various adventures in their village and all over the world. In reality, most historians agree that a real Astérix never existed in Gaul, but in the nearby Roman provinces of Hispania local mountain tribes kept the Roman armies at bay for quite a long time.

If you like the comics, you won't want to miss Parc Astérix, an amusement park just outside of Paris. The park, which recreates the village in the books, has rides, roller-coasters, attractions and live shows as well! There are lots of special effects, some acrobatics, and a few shows with cute animals like dolphins and sea lions.

188

cool, yEaH?

> The first French satellite was named Astérix-1
> in honour of the comic book character.

The Astérix books are available in over 100
languages, including some languages you've
probably never heard of, like Esperanto, Chtimi,
Swabian, Kashubian and Mirandese.

> It's possible that Astérix was inspired by Viriatus,
> 'the terror of the Romans', a tribal leader that led
> the Lusitanian resistance to the Roman armies for a
> whole eight years in the mountains of Lusitania.

Allée des Cygnes
Île des Cygnes. 15ème. and 16ème. Métro: Bir Hakeim, Passy. The Statue of Liberty is at the end of the island, in Pont de Grenelle.

Aquaboulevard Paris
4 – 6 rue Louis Armand. 15ème. Métro: Balard. Tel Tel +33 (0)140601000, www.aquaboulevard.com. Hours: Mon-Fri 9am-11pm (Fri until 12midnight), Sat 8am-12midnight, Sun 8am-11pm. Adult €25, Children (3-11) €10. Shorts-type bathing suits are not allowed – proper swimming gear must be worn (like those of professional swimmers, Speedos for instance).

Aquarium Sea Life Paris
Centre Commercial Val d'Europe, 14, cours du Danube – Serris, Marne la Vallée. RER: Val d'Europe. Tel +33 (0)160423366, www.sealife.fr. Hours: Daily 10am-5:30pm. Adult €15, Children (3-11) €11, Children (under 3) Free.

Arab World Institute
1, rue des Fossés Saint-Bernard, Place Mohammed V. 5ème. Métro: Jussieu, Cardinal-Lemoine, Sully-Morland. Tel +33 (0)140513838, www.imarabe.org. Hours: Tues-Sun 10am-6pm. Museum: Adults €4, Children €4, Children (under 12) Free. Exhibits: Adults €8, Youth (12-26) €6, Children (under 12) Free. There are security measures in place, including metal detectors and personal searches where necessary (mandatory before entering the building).

Arc de Triomphe
Place Charles-de-Gaulle. 8ème. Métro: Charles de Gaule Étoile. Tel +33 (0)155377377, www.arc-de-triomphe.monuments-nationaux.fr. Hours: Apr-Sept: Daily 10am-11pm, Oct-Mar: Daily 10am-10:30pm. Adults €9, Children (under 18) Free. Narrow, steep stairs to the top, elevator available for handicap or elderly people, and parents with small children.

AROUND PARIS
Traditional French Car Tour Tel +33 (0)664504419, www.parisauthentic.com. Hours: 10am-11pm. Adults €30 & up, Children (under 12) Free. Check website for tours and prices. **Batobus** See Boat Tours. **RATP (Métro & RER)** www.ratp.fr. €1,60/ticket. The cheapest deal: €11,40/10 tickets (use 1 per trip, including all train changes). 1, 2, 3 & 5-day passes: Adults €8,80-€28,30 and up, Children (4-11) €4,40-€14,15 & up. **Helicopter Tours** www.heliclass.com. **Velib'** www.velib.paris.fr. 1-day pass €1 or 7-day pass €5 Plus additional charge per half hour of use. Must be over 14 years of age. Credit card required. **Walks** www.pariswater.com.

Les Arts Décoratifs
107, rue Rivoli. 1er. Métro: Palais-Royal Musée du Louvre, Tuileries. Tel +33 (0)144555750, www.lesartsdecoratifs.fr. Hours: Tues-Fri 11am-6pm (Thurs until 9pm), Sat-Sun 10am-6pm. Adults €8, Children (under 18) Free. Audio guide included. Extra charges for temporary exhibitions and Musée Nissim de Camondo.

Atout Branches Park
Route de boutigny, Milly-la-forêt. Tel +33 (0)672468644, www.atoutbranches.com. Hours: Mar-Nov: Sat-Sun10am-7pm; Wed 1pm-7pm. Adult €21, Children (under 15) €18, Children (below 1.4m) €12. Kids get to climb every sort of place, properly geared and hooked for security.

BOAT TOURS
Most companies offer a variety of tours, including sightseeing and lunch/dinner cruises. Hours are seasonal. Check websites for details. **Bateaux Mouches** Port de la Conférence. 8ème. Métro: Alma-Marceau; RER: Pont de l'Alma. Tel +33 (0)142259610, www.bateaux-mouches.fr. Adults €10 & up, Children (under 12) €5 & up, Children (under 4) Free. **Bateaux Parisiens** Port de la

Bourdonnais 7ème. Métro: Bir-Hakeim, Trocadéro; RER: Champ de Mars. Tel +33 (0)176641445, www.bateauxparisiens.com. Adults €11 & up, Children (3-12) €5 & up, Children (under 3) Free. **Batobus** water bus www.batobus. com. 1-day pass: Adults €12, Children (under 16) €6; 2-day (consecutive) pass: Adults €14, Children (under 16) €7; 5-day (consecutive) pass: Adults €17, Children (under 16) €8. **Canauxrama** (1) Place de la Bastille. 12ème. Métro: Bastille. (2) Jaurès. 19ème. Métro: Jaurès. Tel +33 (0)142391500, www.canauxrama.com. Adults € 15 & up, Children (4-12) €8 & up, Children (under 4) Free. **Paris Canal** (1) Port de Solférino. 7ème. Métro: Solférino; RER: Musée d'Orsay. (2) Parc de la Villette. 19ème. Métro: Porte de Pantin. Tel +33 (0)142409697, www.pariscanal.com. Adults €17 & up, Children (4-11) €10 & up. Reservations required. **Vedettes de Paris** Port de Suffren. 7ème. Métro: Bir-Hakeim, Trocadéro; RER: Champ de Mars. Tel +33 (0)144181950 , www.vedettesdeparis.com. Adults €11 & up, Children (4-12) €5 & up, Children (under 4) Free. Pétunia cruise geared toward children aged 4-11. Adults €11, Children (4-12) €7. **Vedettes du Pont Neuf** Place du Vert Galant. 6ème. Métro: Pont Neuf, Louvre; RER: Châtelet, St-Michel. Tel +33 (0)146339838, www.vedettesdupontneuf.com. 1-hour cruise: Adults €12, Children (4-12) €6.

Bois de Boulogne
16ème. Métro: Porte Dauphine; RER: Avenue Foch. Daily. Free.

Bois de Vincennes
12ème. Métro: Porte Dorée, Château de Vincennes. www.boisdevincennes. com. Hours: Daily. Free. Extra charges for Parc Floral, Zoo and Château.

CABARET & VARIETÉ
There are many cabarets in Paris; these three do accept kids. **Lido** 116bis, ave des Champs-Élysées. 8ème. Métro: George V; RER: Charles de Gaulle Etoile. Tel +33 (0)140765610, www.lido.fr. Hours: Daily – check website for showtimes. Adults €80 & up, Children €20-30. Children's menu available at 7pm. **La Nouvelle Eve** 25, rue Fontaine. 18ème. Métro: Blanche. Tel (0)148746925, www.lanouvelleeve.com. Contact for shows, times and prices. **Moulin Rouge** 82, bd de Clichy. 18ème. Métro: Blanche. Tel +33 (0)153098282, www.moulinrouge.fr. Hours: Daily 9pm & 11pm. Adults €89-99, Children (under 12) €44,50-49,50. Extra charge for dinner. Photos not permitted. If attending with children, please contact the Moulin Rouge.

Carnavalet Museum
23, rue de Sévigné. 3ème. Métro: Chemin Vert, Saint-Paul. Tel +33 (0)144595858, www.carnavalet.paris.fr. Hours: Tues-Sun 10am-5:40pm. Free. Extra charge for temporary exhibits. Self-guided neighbourhood tour, kids activities and kids brochures available.

Catacombs of Paris
1, av du Colonel Henri Rol-Tanguy. 14ème. Métro & RER: Denfert-Rochereau. Tel +33 (0)143224763, www.catacombes-de-paris.fr. Hours: Tues-Sun 10am-5pm. Adults €7, Seniors €5,50, Youth (14-26) €3,50, Children (13 and under) Free. The catacombs are age appropriate, but parents should use discretion with more sensitive kids: human skulls are visible, and the place is dark and underground (route is one way only).

Centre Pompidou
Place Georges Pompidou. 4ème. Métro: Rambuteau. Tel +33 (0)144781233, www.centrepompidou.fr. Hours: Daily 11am-9pm. Adults €10-€12, Youth (18-25) €8-€9, Children (under 18) Free. First Sunday of each month free. Shows, concerts and cinema are extra. Children's workshops are held on Wednesdays and Saturdays. Sundays are family days.

Champs-Élysées
8ème. Métro: Concorde, Champs-Élysées Clemenceau, Franklin D. Roosevelt, George V, Charles de Gaulle-Étoile.

Chartres (Tourism)
Place de la Cathédrale. Tel +33 (0)237182626, www.chartres-tourisme.com.

Château de Fontainebleau
Fontainebleau, Tel +33 (0)160715070, www.musee-chateau-fontainebleau. fr. Hours: Apr-Sept: Wed-Mon 9:30am-6pm, Oct-Mar: Wed-Mon 9:30am-5pm. Adults €8, Children (under 18) Free. First Sunday of each month free.

Château de Versailles
RER: Versailles-Rive Gauche. Tel +33 (0)130837800, www.chateauversailles. fr. Hours: Nov-Mar: Tues-Sun 9am-5:30pm, Apr-Oct: Tues-Sun 9am-6:30pm. Full Pass: Adults €16-€20, Children (under 18) Free. Palace Ticket: Adults €13,50, Children (under 18) Free. See website for Marie-Antoinette's Estate, Grand Trianon and Garden hours and fees.

Cinéaqua
5, Avenue Albert De Mun. 16ème. Métro: Trocadéro; RER: Champ de Mars. Tel +33 (0)140692323, www.cineaqua.com. Hours: Daily 10am-8pm. Adults €19,50, Seniors €15,50, Youth (13-17) €15,50, Children (3-12) €12,50, Children (under 3) Free. Ticket is for the day – you can enter and leave throughout the day.

CIRCUS IN PARIS
Cirque d'Hiver Bouglione 110, rue Amelot. 11ème. Métro: Filles du Calvaire, Oberkampf, Republique. Tel +33 (0)147002881, www.cirquedhiver.com. Hours: Variable – check website for showtimes. €10-€45. **Cirque Diana Moreno Bormann** 112, rue de la Haie Coq. 19ème. Tel +33 (0)164053625, www. cirque-diana-moreno.com. Hours: Wed, Sat, Sun 3pm.

City of Immigration History
Palais de la Porte Dorée, 293, ave Daumesnil. 12ème. Métro: Porte Dorée. Tel +33 (0)153595860, www.histoire-immigration.fr. Hours: Tues-Fri 10am-5:30pm; Sat-Sun 10am-7pm. Adults €3-€5, Children (under 18) Free. Age-appropriate guided tour guides available. There is a free booklet for kids visiting with families with questions, games, drawings and word definitions – kids can work on it themselves but may need some help with certain sections. Workshops about 'The Foreigner', memories, departures and displacements - 1.5 hours visit plus 30 min workshop.

City of Music
221, av Jean-Jaurès. 19ème. Métro: Porte de Pantin. Tel +33 (0)144844500, www.cite-musique.fr. Hours: Tues-Sat noon-6pm; Sun 10am-6pm. Museum: Adults €8, Children (under 18) Free. Guided tours are available every Saturday and Sunday at 3pm. There is an extra charge.

City of Science and Industry
30, avenue Corentin-Cariou. 19ème. Métro: Porte de la Villette. Tel +33 (0)140057000, www.cite-sciences.fr. Hours: Tues-Sun 10am-6pm (Sun until 7pm). Adults €6-€15,50, Children €6-€14. Extra charge for some exhibits and attractions.

Conciergerie
2, boulevard du Palais. 1er. Métro: Cité; RER: St-Michel Notre-Dame. Tel +33 (0)153406080, www.conciergerie.monuments-nationaux.fr. Hours: Mar-Oct: Daily 9:30am-6pm, Nov-Feb: Daily 9am-5pm. Adults €6,50, Children (under 18) Free. Children's visit Wednesdays at 2:30 where you can touch items. Laminated information sheets are available for all rooms.

COAST OF NORMANDY

See **Normandy Tourism**: www.normandie-tourisme.fr, www.normandie-pays.
com, www.deauville-normandie-tourisme.com. **D-Day**: www.normandy1944.
com, www.overlordtour.com. **Caen**: www.tourisme.caen.fr. **Le Havre**: www.
lehavretourisme.com. **Honfleur**: www.ot-honfleur.fr. **Mont Saint-Michel**: www.
ot-montsaintmichel.com. **Deauville**: www.deauville.org. **Etretat**: www.etretat.
net.

Disneyland Resort Paris

Marne-la-Vallée, RER: Marne-la-Vallée – Chessy. Tel +33 (0)160306030, www.
disneylandparis.com. Hours: Seasonal; Daily 10am-7pm or longer. Walt Disney
Studios closes earlier. Adults €60, Children (3-11) €52 (1-day, 2 park pass).
1-day, 1 park pass available and 2, 3, 4 & 5-day passes available.

Eiffel Tower

7ème. Métro: Bir-Hakeim, Dupleix, Trocadéro, École Militaire; RER: Champ
de Mars-Tour Eiffel. Tel +33 (0)144112323, www.tour-eiffel.fr. Hours: Daily
9:30am-11:45pm (Jun-Aug: Daily 9am-12:45am). Adults €4,80-12, Children
(3-11) €2,50-6,70.

Fami Parc

D 403, Nonville. Tel +33 (0)164290202, www.fami-parc.com. Hours: Spring
10:30am-6pm, Summer 10:30am-7pm, Autumn 11am-5pm. Seasonal: Adults
€15-€16, Seniors €7-€12, Children (3-11) €13-€14.

Fashion Week

www.modeaparis.com/va/dates/index.html. Check website for dates and
locations.

FLEA MARKETS

Puces de St-Ouen Métro: Porte de Clignancourt. Sat-Mon 9:30am-6pm (don't
arrive too early, since most shops open slowly). Many shops are closed in
August. **Puces de la Porte de Vanves** ave Georges Lafenestre & ave Marc
Sangnier. 14ème. Métro: Porte-de-Vanves. pucesdevanves.typepad.com.
Sat-Sun 7am-1pm (the afternoon market is for new clothing and household
items). **Marché Beauvau** Place d'Aligre. 12ème. Métro: Ledru-Rollin. Tues-Sat
8am-1pm & 4pm-7:30pm, Sun 8am-1pm. **Marché aux Puces de Montreuil**
ave de la Porte de Montreuil, Montreuil-sous-Bois. Métro: Porte de Montreuil.
Sat-Mon 7:30am-6:00pm. **Orphelins-Apprentis d'Auteuil** 40 Rue la Fontaine.
16ème. Métro: Jasmin. Tel +33 (0)144147575. Mon-Fri & First Sat of month,
2:30pm-6pm. Closed August.

France Miniature

Boulevard André Malraux, Elancourt. Tel +33 (0)130161630, www.
franceminiature.fr. Hours: Seasonal – check website. Adult €17,50-€18,50,
Seniors €15,50-€16,50, Children (4-14) €11,50-€12,50.

Grand Palais

ave Winston Churchill. 8ème. Métro: Champs-Elysées-Clémenceau; RER:
Invalides. www.grandpalais.fr. Check website for event information.

Hôtel de Ville

Place de l'Hôtel de Ville. 4ème. Métro: Hôtel de Ville. Tel +33 (0)142764040.
Open for group visits only. **Salon d'accueil** Tel +33 (0)142764343. Hours:
Mon-Sat 10am-7pm, Sun 2pm-7pm. Free.

Hôtel Nationale des Invalides

129, rue de Grenelle. 7ème. Métro: Latour-Maubourg, Varenne; RER:
Invalides. Tel +33 (0)144423877, www.invalides.org. Hours: Oct-Mar: Daily
10am-5pm, Apr-Sept: Daily 10am-6pm. Adults €8, Children (under 18) Free.

Île Saint-Louis

4ème. Métro: Pont Marie, Sully Morland.

Jacquemart-André Museum
158, bd Haussmann. 8ème. Métro: Miromesnil, Saint Philippe du Roule; RER: Charles de Gaulle-Étoile. Tel +33 (0)145621159, www.musee-jacquemart-andre.com. Hours: Daily 10am-6pm. Adults €10, Children (7-17) €7,30. Activity-puzzle book available for children at the main desk. Special programs available for children. See website for details.

Jardin d'Acclimatation
Bois de Boulogne. 16ème. Métro: Les Sablons. Tel +33 (0)140679082, www.jardindacclimatation.fr. Hours: May-Sept: Daily 10am-7pm, Oct-Apr: Daily 10am-6pm. Adults €2,70, Children €2,70.

Jardin des Plantes
57, rue Cuvier or quai St-Bernard. 5ème. Métro: Gare d'Austerlitz, Jussieu; RER: Gare d'Austerlitz. Tel +33 (0)140795601, www.mnhn.fr. Hours: Daily 8am-5:30pm. Free.

Latin Quarter
5ème., 6ème. Métro: Cluny-La Sorbonne, Maubert Mutualité, Cardinal Lemoine; RER: Luxembourg.

Lenôtre Academy for Young Chefs
Pavillon Élysée Lenôtre, 10, av des Champs-Élysées. 8ème. Métro: Champs-Élysées Clemenceau. Tel +33 (0)142659760, www.lenotre.fr/en/ecoles_lenotre.php. Hours: Children (8-11): Wed 2pm-3:30pm; 4pm-5:30pm, Children (12-17): Wed 2pm-5:30pm. Children (8-11) €40, Children (12-17) €80. Check website or call for availability and schedule. Classes are held in French.

Les Halles
1, rue Pierre-Lescot. 1er. Métro: Les Halles; RER: Châtelet-Les-Halles. Tel +33 (0)145080718, www.paris.fr. Hours: Seasonal – check website. Free. Reservations needed for the Children Adventure Garden (parents not allowed in): www.jardindaventure.fr (photos here: www.accomplir.asso.fr/association/photos/jardin_lalanne/index.php)

Living Horse Museum
Les Grandes Écuries, Château Chantilly, Chantilly. RER: Chantilly. Tel +33 (0)344273180, www.museevivantducheval.fr, www.chateaudechantilly.com. Hours: Museum: Nov-Mar: Mon, Wed-Fri 1pm-5pm, Sat-Sun 10:30am-5:30pm, Apr-Oct: Mon, Wed-Fri 10:30am-5:30pm, Sat-Sun 10:30am-6pm. Château: Wed-Mon 10:30am-5pm, Seasonal – check website for current hours. Museum: Adults €9, Children (4-17) €7. Museum, Château & Park: Adults €17, Children (4-17) €7

Louvre Museum
34-36 quai du Louvre & 99, rue de Rivoli. 1er. Métro: Palais-Royal-Musée du Louvre. Tel +33 (0)144113399, www.louvre.fr. Hours: Wed-Mon 9am-6pm (Wed, Fri until 10pm). Adults €9 (€6 after 6pm). First Sun of month free. Temporary exhibits extra. Wednesday and Friday evenings are the least-crowded. To avoid waiting in long lines, use the Rue de Rivoli entrance, or buy your ticket ahead of time. Various brochures available that showcase themed tours, eg. the Da Vinci Code food/eating; lions(!); the masterpieces of the Louvre; and Christmas.

Luxembourg Garden
bd Saint-Michel. 6ème. Métro: Odéon; RER: Luxembourg. www.paris.fr. Hours: Apr-Oct: Daily 7am-sunset, Nov-Mar: Daily 8am-sunset. Free. Extra charge for some attractions and activities.

Mer de Sable
Ermenonville. Tel +33 (0)825252060, www.merdesable.fr. Hours: Daily 10am-6pm. Adults €19, Children (3-11) €15,50.

Musée d'Orsay
1, rue de la Légion d'Honneur. 7ème. Métro: Assemblée Nationale; RER: Musée d'Orsay. Tel +33 (0)140494814, www.musee-orsay.fr. Hours: Tues-Sun 9:30-6pm (Thurs until 9:45pm). Adults €9,50, Children (under 18) Free. Comined (same day) Musée d'Orsay – Musée Rodin Passport €12. Two-hour workshops for kids – 45 minutes in the gallery, 1:15 of activities in an effort to foster creativity, not learning. Pick up a family tours pamphlet at the entrance – a game lets you explore the museum.

Musée Grévin
10, bd Montmartre. 9ème. Métro: Grands Boulevards. Tel +33 (0)147708505, www.grevin.com. Hours: Mon-Fri 10am-6:30pm, Sat-Sun 10am-7pm. Adults €19,50, Seniors €16,50, Children (6-14) €11,50.

Musée Rodin
79, rue de Varenne. 7ème. Métro: Varenne; RER: Invalides. Tel +33 (0)144186110, www.musee-rodin.fr. Hours: Apr-Sept: Tues-Sun 9:30am-5:45pm (Garden until 6:45pm), Oct-Mar: Tues-Sun 9:30am-4:45pm (Garden until 5pm). Museum: Adults €6, Children (under 18) Free. Comined (same day) Musée d'Orsay – Musée Rodin Passport €12. Garden: €1. Audio guides €4. Workshops – interactive visits for children including games and drawing.

Museum of Air and Space
Airport Le Bourget, Le Bourget. Tel +33 (0)149927062, www.mae.org. Hours: Apr-Sept: Daily 10am-6pm, Oct-Mar: Daily 10am-5pm. Free. Audio guides €3, Boeing 747, Concorde, Planetarium extra. Children under 14 must be accompanied by an adult.

Museum of Arts and Crafts
60, rue Réaumur. 3ème. Métro: Arts-et-Métiers. Tel +33 (0)153018200, www.arts-et-metiers.net. Hours: Tues-Sun 10am-6pm (Thurs until 9:30pm). Adults €6,50, Children (under18) Free. Audio guides €2,50. Extra charge for temporary exhibits. Tours with different themes available.

Museum of Jewish Art and History
71, rue du Temple. 3ème. Métro: Rambuteau, Hôtel de Ville; RER: Châtelet-Les Halles. Tel +33 (0)153018660, www.mahj.org. Hours: Mon-Fri 11am-6pm, Sun 10am-6pm. Adults €6,80, Children (under 18) Free. Extra charge for exhibits. Mandatory security control at entrance. Tours and workshops for children and families available.

Museum of Magic
11, rue Saint Paul. 4ème. Métro: Saint-Paul, Bastille, Sully-Morland. Tel +33 (0)142721326, www.museedelamagie.com. Hours: Wed, Sat, Sun 2pm-7pm. Adults €9, Children €7.

National Museum of Natural History
Jardin des Plantes, 36, rue Geoffroy. 5ème. Métro: Gare d'Austerlitz, Jussieu, Censier Daubenton; RER: Gare d'Austerlitz. Tel +33 (0)140795479, www.nmnh.fr. Hours: Wed-Mon 10am-6pm. Adults €8, Children (4-13) €6.

National Museum of the Middle Ages
6, place Paul Painlevé. 5ème. Métro: Cluny-La Sorbonne. Tel +33 (0)153737800, www.musee-moyenage.fr. Hours: Wed-Mon 9:15am-5:45pm, Adults €7,50, Children (under 18) Free. Audio guides € 1. First Sun of the month free. Ask for a Comme des Images brochure at the entrance – it has information and challenges for kids while visiting. Activities and workshops available by appointment.

Notre Dame de Paris
Cathedral 6 Parvis Notre-Dame, Place Jean-Paul II. 4ème. Métro: Cité; RER: St-Michel Notre-Dame. Tel +33 (0)142345610, www.notredamedeparis.fr.

Hours: Mon-Fri 8am-6:45pm; Sat-Sun 8am-7:15pm. Free. Tower and the Crypt rue du cloître Notre-Dame. 4ème. Métro: Cité; RER: St-Michel Notre-Dame. Tel +33 (0)153100700, www.notre-dame-de-paris.monuments-nationaux.fr. Hours: Apr-Sept: Daily 10am-6:30pm, Oct-Mar: Daily 10am-5:30pm. Adults €7,50, Children (under 18) Free.

Open Air Sculpture Museum
quai St-Bernard. 5ème. Métro: Gare d'Austerlitz. Hours: Daily. Free.

OPÉRA
Palais Garnier 8, rue Scribe. 9ème. Métro: Opéra; RER: Auber. Tel +33 (0)172293535, www.operadeparis.fr. Hours: Daily 10am-5pm. Adults €8, Youth (10-24) €4, Children (under 10) Free. Guided tours available for an extra charge. Check website for schedule. **Opéra Bastille** 120, rue de Lyon. 12ème. Métro: Bastille. Tel + 33 (0)140011970, www.operadeparis.fr. Hours: Call for tour times. Adults €11, Youth (10-24) €9, Children (under 10) €6. Guided tours only.

Oya Café
25, rue de la Reine Blanche. 13ème. Métro: Les Gobelins. Tel +33 (0)147075959, www.oya.fr. Hours: Tues-Sat 2pm-12midnight (Sun until 9pm).

Palais de Chaillot – Marine Museum
17, pl du Trocadéro. 16ème. Métro: Trocadéro. Tel +33 (0)153656969, www. musee-marine.fr. Hours: Wed-Mon 10am-6pm. Adults €6,50, Children (6-18) €5.

Palais de la Découverte
ave Franklin D. Roosevelt. 8ème. Métro: Franklin D. Roosevelt; RER: Invalides. Tel +33 (0)156432021, www.palais-decouverte.fr. Hours: Tues-Sat 9:30am-6pm, Sun 10am-7pm. Adults €7, Seniors €4,50, Children (under 18) €4,50. Extra charge for Planetarium and for some workshops.

Palais Royal's Gardens
Place du Palais-Royal. 1er. Métro: Palais-Royal-Musée du Louvre. Hours: Daily 7:30am-8:30pm. Free.

Le Panthéon
Place du Panthéon. 5ème. Métro: Cardinal Lemoine; RER: Luxembourg. Tel +33 (0)144321800, www.pantheon.monuments-nationaux.fr. Hours: Apr-Sept: Daily 10am-6:30pm, Oct-Mar: Daily 10am-6pm. Adults €7,50, Children (under 18) Free.

Parc André Citroën
2, rue Cauchy. 15ème. Métro: Javel André Citroën, Balard; RER: Javel. www. paris.fr. Hours: Seasonal – check website. Free. Ballon Air de Paris Tel. +33 (0)144262000, www.ballondeparis.com. Hours: Daily 9am-30 minutes before park closing. Adults: Mon-Fri €10, Sat-Sun €12, Children (12-17): Mon-Fri €9, Sat-Sun €10, Children (3-11): Mon-Fri €5, Sat-Sun €6.

Parc Astérix
Plailly. Tel +33 (0)826301040, www.parcasterix.fr. Hours: Seasonal – check website. Adults €37, Children (3-11) €27.

Parc de la Villette
211, av Jean Jaurès. 19ème. Métro: Porte de Pantin. Tel +33 (0)140037575, www.villette.com. Hours: Daily. Free.

PARIS BERCY
Park of Bercy rue de Bercy. 12ème. Métro: Bercy. Tel +33 (0)153461919. House of gardening has a library and workshops on planting and growing flowers and plants. Free. **Bercy Village** Cour St-Émilion. 12ème. Métro: Cour St-Émilion Tel (0)140029080, www.bercyvillage.com. Shops, activities, parks, restaurants. **Bibliothèque Nationale de France** quai François-Mauriac.

13ème. Métro: Quai de la Gare; RER: Bibliothèque François-Mitterrand. Tel +33 (0)153795959, www.bnf.fr. Reference Library: 1 day pass €3,30. Reference Library open to anyone over 16 years of age. Iconic anchor buildings for the whole Bercy area. Exhibition: Tues-Sat 10am-7pm, Sun 1pm-7pm. Adults €5-7, Children (under 18) Free. Check website for current exhibitions. It is free to visit the BnF grounds. Imax cinema and specialiazed bookstores next door. The computerized metro to Bercy is interesting for younger kids (no driver) – get the front seats!

Paris La Défense
Métro: La Défense; RER: La Défense. **Grande Arche** www.grandearche. com. Hours: Apr-Aug: Daily 10am-8pm; Sept-Mar: Daily 10am-7pm. Adults €10, Children €8,50. Top is open to the public. It also houses the **Museum of Computing** which follows the history of computers since World War II. **Les Quatre Temps** shopping centre. www.les4temps.com. Hours: Mon-Sat 10am-8pm.

Paris Story
11 bis, rue Scribe. 9ème. Métro: Opéra; RER: Auber. Tel +33 (0)142666206, www.paris-story.com. Hours: Daily 10am-7pm. Adults €10, Children (6-18) €6. Shows every hour. A great place to start your visit to Paris.

Père-Lachaise Cemetery
16, rue du Repos. 20e. Métro: Père-Lachaise, Philippe Auguste, Gambetta. Tel +33 (0)155258210, www.pere-lachaise.com. Hours: Mon-Fri 8am-6pm; Sat 8:30am-6pm; Sun 9am-6pm. Free. Tours run on Saturdays at 3pm Jun-Sept. Pick up a map at the conservation office or purchase the Metropolitains Edition map from a vendor just outside the entrance near the Père-Lachaise Métro stop.

Petit Palais
ave Winston Churchill. 8ème. Métro: Champs-Elysées-Clemenceau, Concorde; RER: Invalides, Charles-de-Gaulle-Étoile. Tel +33 (0)153434000, www.petitpalais.paris.fr. Hours: Tues-Sun 10am-6pm. Free.

Place de la Concorde
8ème. Métro: Concorde.

Place des Vosges
4ème. Métro: Chemin-Vert, St-Paul, Bastille.

Place Vendôme
1er. Métro: Tuileries.

Promenade Plantée
12ème. Métro: Bastille, Gare de Lyon, Daumesnil, Dugommier.

PUNCH & JUDY PUPPET SHOWS
Théâtre Guignol Anatole Parc des Buttes-Chaumont in Paris. 19ème. Métro: Laumière. Tel +33 (0)140309760, www.petits-bouffons.com. Apr-Jun: Wed, Sat, Sun – check website. Closed Oct-Apr. Adults €3, Children €3. **Champs de Mars** 7ème. Métro: École Militaire. Tel +33 (0)148560144. Wed, Sat, Sun (most). **Jardin d'Acclimatation** Bois de Boulogne. 16ème. Métro: Sablons. Tel +33 (0)145015352. Wed, Sat, Sun (most). **Jardin du Luxembourg** 6ème. Métro: Vavin. Tel +33 (0)143264647. Wed, Sat, Sun (most).

Quai Branly Museum
37, quai Branly. 7ème. Métro: Alma-Marceau, Bir-Hakeim. Tel +33 (0)156617000, www.quaibranly.fr. Hours: Tues, Wed, Sun 11am-7pm; Thurs-Sat 11am-9pm. Adults €10, Children (under 18) Free. Audio guides €5. The newest of the big Paris museums, Quai Branly offers the best selection of activities for kids and family. The museum has intriguing, curious and scary objects that, by design, force kids to ask many questions. The museum and

garden's architecture are very sensorial. Many workshops are available (mostly in French and receptive to English-speaking kids), including craft making. Seasonal themes. Reservations are required and can be made at +33 (0)156617172. The museum offers a large number of temporary exhibitions during the year, as well as shows, music and cinema. If you are visiting just one museum with kids, make this your choice!

Rollers et Coquillages
Place de la Bastille. 4ème., 11ème., 12ème. Métro: Bastille, (23-25, rue Jean-Jacques Rousseau). Tel +33 (0)144549442, www.rollers-coquillages.org. Hours: Sun 2:30pm-5:30pm. Free. Event starts and ends at Bastille and lasts about 3 hours. Skaters can stop anytime.

Sacré-Cœur de Montmartre
35, rue de Chevalier-de-la-Barre, 18ème. Métro: Anvers, Abbesses. www.sacre-coeur-montmartre.com. Hours: Basilica: Daily 6am-11pm. Free. Dome: Daily 8:30am-6:30pm. Adults €5, Children (6 and up) €5. Visit Montmartre in the early morning – it is very popular with tourists and it gets extremely crowded during the day and on weekends. A funicular takes you up to the church at the top of the hill (1 Métro ticket required) – definitely something to check out, particularly for the view.

Saint-Denis Basilica
1, rue de la Légion d'Honneur, Saint-Denis. Métro: Basilique de Saint-Denis. Tel +33 (0)148098354, www.saint-denis.monuments-nationaux.fr. Hours: Apr-Sept: Mon-Sat 10am-6:15pm; Sun noon-6:15pm, Oct-Mar: Mon-Sat 10am-5pm; Sun noon-5:15pm. Adults €6,50, Children (under 18) Free.

Sainte-Chapelle
4 bd du Palais. 1er. Métro: Cité; RER: St-Michel Notre-Dame. Tel +33 (0)153406080, www.sainte-chapelle.monuments-nationaux.fr. Hours: Mar-Oct: Daily 9:30am-6pm, Nov-Feb: Daily 9am-5pm. Adults €7,50, Children (under 18) Free. There are metal controls and searches at all entrances – be prepared for long cues. Do not bring any metal objects such as knives, scissors or any other pointy or sharp metal objects. Children are generally exempt.

Sewers of Paris
93, quai d'Orsay. 7ème. Métro: Alma-Marceau. Tel +33 (0)153682781, www.paris.fr. Hours: Oct-Apr: Sat-Wed 11am-4pm, May-Sept: Sat-Wed 11am-5pm. Adults €4,20, Children (6-16) €3,40, Children (under 6) Free.

Stade de France (Tours)
93216, Saint Denis La Plaine. Métro: Saint-Denis Porte de Paris; RER: Stade de France, Saint-Denis, La Plaine Stade de France. Tel +33 (0)155930000, www.stadefrance.com. Hours: Tours at 10:30am, 12noon, 2:30pm, 4:30pm. Adults €12, Children (6-18) €8, Children (under 6) Free, Family €32. Tour lasts about 60 minutes. In French with English guidebook available at the shop for €6. Matches/games extra (no tours on match days).

Tour de France
www.letour.fr. The Tour de France takes place over 3 weeks in July. The route changes every year, although the race always ends on the Champs-Élysées. Check website for dates and locations.

Tour Montparnasse
33, ave du Maine. 14ème. Métro: Montparnasse-Bienvenüe, Edgar Quinet; RER: Denfert-Rochereau. Tel +33 (0)145385256, www.tourmontparnasse56.com. Hours: Apr-Sept: Daily 9:30am-11:30pm, Oct-Mar: Sun-Thurs 9:30am-10:30pm, Fri-Sat 9:30am-11pm. Adults €10, Children (7-15) €4,50, Children (6 and under) Free.

Tuileries Garden
rue de Rivoli. 1er. Métro: Tuileries, Palais Royal. www.paris.fr. Hours:
Seasonal. Free.
Zoo de Vincennes
Bois de Vincennes, ave de Saint-Maurice. 12ème. Métro: Porte Dorée. Tel +33
(0)144752000, www.boisdevincennes.com/site/zoo.php3. Hours: Summer:
9am-6pm, Winter: 9am-5pm. Adults €8, Children (4-16) €5.

child-FRiENdly HoTEl pick

Hôtel de Fleurie * * *
32 rue Grégoire de Tours, 75006 Paris. Tel +33 (0)1.5373.7000
Fax +33 (0)1.5373.7020 Email: bonjour@hotel-de-fleurie.fr
www.hoteldefleurie.fr. This is a simply decorated, no-fuss quiet
family-run hotel in the heart of Saint-Germain-des-Près, in the
Left Bank. The spacious connecting rooms make it a perfect,
comfortable pick for a stay with
kids (those under 12 stay free
with the parents). Within 5 minutes
from this 18th century building are
Montparnasse, the Luxemboug
Garden and the River Seine, etc.
The metro is also on the doorstep.

REcomMENdEd apaRtMENt SERvicEs

Hotels in central Paris can be extremely expensive in any
season. Renting an apartment, especially when you are
travelling with kids, is a great option. The added freedom
(and room) will make the stay that much more enjoyable...
but also cheaper. Apartments of all sizes, locations, and
prices are widely available in all
styles (from rustic to sleek, and
every styles in-between). Paris
Attitude is a good, reliable service
(**www.parisattitude.com**). Prices
for 4 people start as low as
500 euro/week, increasing
gradually as the arrondissement
number decreases.

199

a littlE fRENcH:
caN you Say RatafouillE?

In French, you must address adults and kids with a different word. For adults you should always use 'vous', and for kids you should always use 'tu'. Easy, easy!

Hello / Hi = Salut
Yes / No = oui / NoN

Goodbye = au REvoiR / adiEu
Good morning / Good afternoon = boNjouR
Good evening / Good night = boNsoiR

Please = S'il tE plait / S'il vous plait
Thank you (very much) = mERci (biEN)
You're welcome = dE RiEN / jE vous EN pRiE
Excuse me / Sorry = ExcusE moi / ExcusEz moi

HOW TO INTRODUCE YOURSELF

What's your name?
= commENt t'appEllEs tu?
/ vous appElEz-vous?
My name is... = jE m'appEllE...
Pleased to meet you
= ENcHaNtE
How are you?
= commENt ça va?
Fine thanks, and you?
= biEN, mERci. Et tu / vous?
See you later = a biENtot!

I am American / Canadian / English = jE
jE suis amERicaiN / caNadiEN / aNGlais

200

COMMUNICATING

Do you speak English? = paRlEs-tu aNGlais?
/ paRlEz-vous aNGlais?

I speak very little French
= jE NE paRlE pas bEaucoup dE fRançais

I understand = jE compREnds
I don't understand = jE NE compREnds pas

Could you repeat that, please?
= Est-cE quE tu pEuX / vous pouvEz
REpEtER. s'il tE plait / vous plait?

USEFUL LINES AROUND AMSTERDAM

Can you help me?
= tu pEuX / vous pouvEz m'aidER?

I'd like... (something) = jE voudRais...

What time is it? = quEl hEuRE Est-il?

How much does this cost? = c'Est combiEN?

Where is the toilet?
= lEs toilEttEs sont ou?

A ticket to... , please
= uN billEt pouR... s'il vous plait.

Is this the right way to...?
= c'Est la boNNE RoutE pouR allER...?

RatatouillE
= a typical French vegetable stew... and a cooking rat!

Photograph credits and copyrights (clockwise from top left):